THE WHICH? GUIDE TO
GIVING AND INHERITING

THE WHICH? GUIDE TO GIVING AND INHERITING

Jonquil Lowe

CONSUMERS' ASSOCIATION

Which? Books are commissioned by
The Association for Consumer Research
and published by Consumers' Association
2 Marylebone Road, London NW1 4DF

Distributed by The Penguin Group:
Penguin Books Ltd, 27 Wrights Lane, London W8 5TZ

Typographic design by Paul Saunders
Cover photographs by courtesy of ACE Photo Agency/
Martin Lipscombe/John Panton/Carroll Seghers II

First edition October 1992
Revised edition June 1994
Copyright © 1994 Consumers' Association Ltd

A catalogue record for this book is available from the British Library

ISBN 0 85202 570 X

Typeset by FMT Colour Ltd
Printed and bound in Great Britain by
Clays Ltd, St Ives plc, Bungay, Suffolk

Contents

Introduction 7

1 Gifts and taxes 9

PART 1: GIVING TO CHARITY

2 Choosing the charities 17
3 Special schemes for giving to charity 25
4 Other ways of giving to charity 35
Appendix to Part 1: Summary of gifts to charity 45

PART 2: LIFETIME GIFTS TO FAMILY AND FRIENDS

5 Tax-free gifts 49
6 Capital gains tax on lifetime gifts 59
7 Inheritance tax on lifetime gifts 73
8 Income tax and gifts 87
9 Using trusts 95

PART 3: INHERITANCE

10 Making a will 111
11 Tax at the time of death 125
12 Inheritance planning 141
Appendix to Part 3: Rates of inheritance tax 1986–92 155
Glossary 157
Useful addresses 167
Bibliography 169
Index 171

Introduction

Giving is easy, but making sure that your gifts reach the people you choose, and that they are used as you would like, is not quite so straightforward. However, you can avoid disappointments and problems by planning ahead.

Around three-quarters of the British population give away money to charities,[1] and most people also make personal gifts to family and friends. Few of us would put the Inland Revenue high on our list of worthy recipients, yet year after year tax relief on some gifts is ignored and other gifts are needlessly wrapped in a tax bill. With some planning, you can use the tax system to increase the value of your giving.

Similarly, when we pass on wealth to our heirs, there may be a tax bill which could have been avoided with a little forethought. But tax is not the only problem: it is estimated that only three out of ten adults have made a will.[2] Without a will, it is not just the Inland Revenue who might be your lucky heir – your children might inherit at the expense of your spouse, or your wealth could all end up with estranged relatives instead of the family close to you.

Planning ahead has another advantage too: it can give you some control over how your gifts are used. Whether you are making gifts now or looking ahead at inheritance, using special legal arrangements or particular investments can help to ensure that your gifts are used largely as you wish. This can be especially useful where children are concerned.

[1] Charities Aid Foundation (CAF). 1992. *Individual giving and volunteering in Britain*. 5th edn. Tonbridge, CAF.
[2] 'Making your will' in *Which?*, Consumers' Association, June 1991.

Through clear explanation and over 40 examples, this book will act as your guide to planned and efficient donations to charities, gifts to family, gifts to friends, and inheritance under your will.

Information in this book generally applies to UK residents making gifts to people, charities and other organisations which are based in the United Kingdom. In some cases, the rules for Scotland and Northern Ireland differ from those for the rest of the United Kingdom; where possible, this has been indicated, but details of the different systems are outside the scope of this book.

Changes up to and including the November 1993 Budget have been taken into account, although at the time of writing the November 1993 Budget changes have yet to be made law and could be subject to alteration.

CHAPTER 1

GIFTS AND TAXES

Gifts to charity

It is a fortunate paradox that people are willing to give to total strangers through the medium of charities. But, while it is not so odd that we care about, and want to help, with such matters as poverty, suffering, the global standard of living, protecting culture, bio-diversity and saving the environment, it is surely very strange that many people ignore the encouragement which the government offers to charitable giving in the form of tax reliefs.

Estimates suggest that the British population gave between £3.5 billion and £4.3 billion to charity in the year to August 1991.[3] Of this, it is likely that nearly half was unplanned giving in response to collections, TV and postal appeals, advertisements by charities, and the like.[4] This means that between £1.6 billion and £2 billion was given without taking advantage of any of the tax reliefs available – a loss to charities of some £500 million or more.

With the government planning to shift even more responsibility from the public to the voluntary sector,[5] and with the persistent problems of droughts and wars in many regions of the world, voluntary donations to charities are likely to be ever more important. It is all the more pressing, therefore, to stop and think about your own charitable giving. Could you plan ahead? For example, could you give fewer larger sums rather than many small donations? Or could you commit yourself to giving regularly? If so, your gifts can be arranged so that the government will add to them and make them

---

[3]CAF. 1992. *Individual giving and volunteering in Britain*. 5th edn. Tonbridge, CAF.
[4]*Ibid*. Table 2.6.
[5]Government statement made on 19 February 1992.

even more effective. Furthermore, gifts to charities can often directly save you tax as well, if they are planned.

Part 1 of this book looks at the range of charitable gifts which may qualify for the available tax reliefs and shows you how to use the special schemes for giving to charity.

Gifts to family and friends

Giving to people you know is not so paradoxical. Most people see themselves as part of a social group and care about the well-being of its members. The most intimate circle is the family, and here there is a natural desire to pass on wealth, particularly from one generation to another.

The distribution of wealth

Left unchecked, inheritance within families would, sooner or later, lead to a concentration of wealth in the hands of relatively few people. However, most advanced societies take the view that wealth should not be distributed too unevenly. The reasons for this are varied – political, economic, but also humane. A wide gulf between the poorest people and the richest may encourage political unrest; the votes of relatively poorer people can perhaps be 'bought' by redistributing wealth to them. Economic activity may be improved if wealth is spread more evenly, because of the different spending and saving patterns of the rich and poor.

But there are less pragmatic reasons too. The majority of people want to accumulate enough possessions and wealth to support an enjoyable and sustainable life-style, but not while ignoring the relative, or absolute, poverty of others. Our sense of justice demands that others should also have the chance of a reasonable life.

Yet, even in a society as mature as that of the United Kingdom, the distribution of wealth across the population is remarkably uneven, as Table 1.1 shows. Just one-tenth of the adult population in the United Kingdom owns over half of all the wealth, and a quarter of the population own three-quarters of all the wealth.

However, the distribution of wealth is now more even than it was in the early part of the century (see Table 1.2). This partly reflects the effect of governments' redistribution policies.

Table 1.1 Who owns what in the United Kingdom

Percentage of population[1]	Percentage of wealth owned[2]
1	17
2	25
5	38
10	53
25	75
50	94

Notes: [1]Percentage of the most wealthy of the UK adult population.
[2]Percentage of marketable wealth excluding pension rights.
Source: *Inland Revenue Statistics*, London, HMSO, 1990, figures for 1988.

Table 1.2 Changing fortunes

Year	Percentage of wealth[1] owned by the wealthiest 1%[2]	Percentage of wealth[1] owned by the wealthiest 10%[2]
1911–13	69	92
1924–30	62	91
1936–38	56	88
1954	43	79
1960	38	77
1966	32	72
1972	30	72
1978	20	49
1984	18	48
1988	17	53

Notes: [1]Percentage of marketable wealth excluding pension rights.
[2]Percentage of the most wealthy of the UK adult population.
Source: *Diamond Commission Initial Report on the Distribution of Income and Wealth*, London, HMSO, 1975; *Inland Revenue Statistics*, London, HMSO, 1990

The main tool which governments use to influence the distribution of wealth is the tax system. There are several ways in which taxes can be used to 'take from the rich'. One obvious way might be to tax people regularly on the amount of wealth they have. Wealth taxes are used in some countries and have been proposed for the United Kingdom in the past.[6] At present in the United Kingdom,

[6]*Wealth Tax*, Labour government green paper. 1974. London, HMSO.

however, there is no tax on simply *owning* wealth. Instead, the emphasis is on taxing wealth as it changes hands.

Taxing wealth and gifts

Originally, taxing the transfer of wealth was confined to a tax at the time of death and can be traced back to the Anglo-Saxon 'heriot' – a feudal tax paid to the local lord on the death of a tenant. But the modern form of this type of taxation started with estate duty introduced in 1894 with a swingeing top rate of 8 per cent!

Although estate duty aimed mainly to tax the passing on of wealth at the time of death, it also taxed gifts made in the few years before death to close an otherwise obvious loophole: that is, avoiding the tax through last minute 'death-bed bequests'. Even so, with planning, it was possible to avoid the worst ravages of the estate duty, particularly by giving away wealth during lifetime.

In 1975, Harold Wilson's government scrapped estate duty in favour of capital transfer tax. This was a fully fledged gifts tax and estate duty rolled into one. The aim was to tax all transfers of wealth whether made in life or at death – with a few exceptions, such as gifts between husband and wife, small gifts to other people, and up to £2,000 a year (in the 1975–76 tax year) of otherwise taxable transfers. And there were special reliefs to help farmers and businesses. Taxable gifts were added together and the first slice of this total was tax-free. Tax, at progressively higher rates, was levied on subsequent slices until it reached a top rate of 75 per cent. Although this looked to be a serious tax that would affect even people of relatively modest means, in the event, capital transfer tax lasted only 11 years.

The Conservative government came to power in 1979 determined to reduce the role of the state and to encourage individual initiative. Reform of the tax system was an important part of its strategy, and capital transfer tax was on the agenda. In 1986, capital transfer tax was replaced by inheritance tax. In many respects the two taxes are similar, but a major difference is that under the inheritance tax regime most lifetime gifts between people are free from tax, apart from gifts made in the last seven years before the death of the giver. This means that most gifts made in the course of your day-to-day affairs are not caught up in the inheritance tax net.

You may need to watch out for other taxes though. When you give away something (other than cash), you have 'disposed' of it – just as if you had sold it. If the value of the thing has risen since you first acquired it, you will be judged to have made a profit from owning it and there may be capital gains tax to pay – even though you did not actually receive the profit yourself! And income which you give away can sometimes be like a boomerang which keeps coming back to haunt your tax assessments.

Part 2 examines the various taxes you need to watch out for when making gifts in your lifetime and looks at how to arrange your gifts tax efficiently. In addition, it discusses using 'trusts' (special legal arrangements), which can be a way of giving something but retaining some control over how the gift is used. Contrary to popular opinion, trusts are not just for the very wealthy; they can be useful even if you have fairly small sums to give.

As with charitable giving, the pitfalls of the taxes on gifts to family and friends can often be avoided if you plan ahead. Nowhere is this more crucial than in the area of inheritance planning. The first step is, of course, to make a will – though seven out of ten people do not even take this step.[7] Yet, without a will, your possessions may not reach the people you want to leave them to and you lose a chance to plan away a possible tax bill.

Part 3 considers the problems of estates where no will is made, explains how gifts made at the time of death are taxed, and shows some steps which can be taken to help you develop an effective plan for giving. In the last resort, it may even be possible for your heirs to rearrange gifts made to them under your will (or in accordance with the law if you left no will) and Part 3 also takes a look at how these measures work.

---

[7]'Making your will' in *Which?*, Consumers' Association, June 1991.

PART 1

GIVING TO CHARITY

CHAPTER 2

CHOOSING THE CHARITIES

IS IT A CHARITY?

'How odd,' said Mary, as she joined the rest of the family around the tea table, 'That phone call was from a man saying he was collecting money for a charity and would I make a donation over the phone with my credit card.'

Mary and Philip support several charities: they respond to regular postal appeals from Help the Aged, buy Christmas gifts through a Save the Children catalogue, belong to the National Trust, and often seek out bargains in the local charity shop. It is likely that their names are on various lists which are passed on to other charities, so Mary was not surprised to be contacted out of the blue. 'But I didn't like to give anything,' she said. 'I've never heard of the charity – though he did say it was registered, whatever that means. I had no way of knowing whether he was genuine . . .'

What is a charity?

Charities are part of the 'voluntary sector' of the economy. The voluntary sector is made up of a very diverse range of organisations – from youth clubs to poverty relief groups, from fête committees to conservation groups – whose aim is to benefit some specified group or groups of people, or society as a whole. Often voluntary groups are run by lowly paid or unpaid volunteers, but others are large, highly organised concerns with paid workers and well-developed management systems. Voluntary groups often rely on fund-raising, gifts or grants for their finance.

Charities are distinct from the rest of the voluntary sector because they benefit from special tax status which makes them largely exempt from most taxes. There are thought to be around 270,000 charities in England and Wales.[8] In order to be a charity, an organisation must show that its purposes fall into at least one of the following broad areas:[9]

- the relief of poverty
- the advancement of education
- the advancement of religion
- the pursuit of other aims which are judged beneficial to the community

It is easy to think of examples of charities helping to relieve poverty that fit the first category: Oxfam, Save the Children, Shelter, Help the Aged and so on. People are often surprised, however, at what counts as a charity in the other categories. For example, which of the following do *you* think are charities: ASH, Amnesty International, The Royal Opera House, the 'Moonies'? Table 2.1 gives you the answers; it shows the results of a survey carried out by *Which?* magazine to test its subscribers' perception of which organisations were charities.

The second category of charities – the promotion of education – is not to be confused with education itself; its scope is much wider and it can cover virtually any field, including medical research, and making available musical and sporting activities, as well as actively passing on skills and knowledge. For example, this category covers charities as diverse as Imperial Cancer Research Fund, the Royal Opera House, Covent Garden, British Red Cross Society, and Action on Smoking and Health (ASH), as well as more obviously educational bodies such as the Pre-school Playgroups Association (PPA) and a number of schools.

The third category includes bodies such as the Salvation Army, Church Missionary Society, and churches themselves. The final

---

[8] *1991 Report of the Charity Commissioners for England and Wales*, London: HMSO, 1992; *Charities: a framework for the future*, Government white paper. May 1989. London, HMSO

[9] The division into these broad areas is known as the 'Macnaghten doctrine' after the judge who first defined them.

Table 2.1 *Which?* subscribers' perception of what counts as a charity

Subscribers were asked: which of the following do you think are registered charities?	Percentage of responses			Correct answer
	Yes	No	Don't know	
National Trust	68	16	14	Yes
The Unification Church 'Moonies'	28	47	23	Yes
Anti-apartheid movement	6	54	37	No
Royal Opera House, Covent Garden	27	35	35	Yes
Child Poverty Action Group	73	7	19	Yes
National Anti-Vivisection Society	33	25	39	No
Shelter	82	4	12	Yes
Howard League for Penal Reform	26	20	52	Yes
Eton College	18	47	32	Yes
Action on Smoking & Health (ASH)	21	38	38	Yes
Lord's Day Observance Society	21	30	46	Yes
National Canine Defence League	57	10	30	Yes
Amnesty International	50	17	30	No

Source: *Which?* questionnaire, unpublished, 1990.

category enables charitable status to be given to bodies such as the National Trust, Worldwide Fund for Nature and the Royal Society for the Prevention of Cruelty to Animals (RSPCA).

Organisations whose aims are partly or wholly political cannot be charities, even if part of their work falls into one or more of the categories above. This is why, for example, Amnesty International does not qualify for charitable status. But this does not mean that charities have to be totally apolitical. A charity is allowed to try to influence political decisions, but only in the course of pursuing its charitable aims, and it must not be too pro-active in the means it chooses. Providing information and argument is acceptable, but acting as a pressure group is not. This is a grey area and even well-established charities can fall foul of the rules: for example, in 1991, Oxfam was warned that some of its campaigning to relieve distress and suffering in areas such as the Middle East and South Africa had unwittingly strayed too far over the line and amounted to advocating political change, and that in future they would have to curb such political activities.

What does 'registered' mean?

In general, charities must be registered with the Charity Commission, which is a government body responsible for checking that an organisation's purposes really are charitable, investigating abuse (for example, fraud, or negligent use of charitable funds), and helping charities to operate effectively. But, contrary to popular belief, not all charities must be, or indeed are, 'registered charities'.

Becoming registered is not the same as being granted charitable status. Many types of charities are excluded from the need to register but are still able to benefit from the special tax status. They include universities, voluntary schools, churches, and many very small charities (for whom the administrative burden of registration would be ridiculously great given the scale of their activities). There are some 166,500 'registered charities',[10] but a further 100,000 or so which are not registered.[11]

Checking out charity collections

Charities raise funds in a wide range of ways: street collections, door-to-door collections, donation boxes in shops and pubs, sponsorships, postal appeals, TV appeals, even telephone appeals.

Though the amounts given are generally small, door-to-door and street collections are probably the most commonly used methods of giving to charity.[12] Whereas you might discard an appeal letter, say, it is hard to refuse a direct appeal for a small donation, even if you have never heard of the particular charity. So, how can you be sure that the collection is genuinely for charity?

If people arrive at your door collecting money, they must by law carry a Certificate of Authority identifying themselves and the purpose of the collection. Similarly, street collectors must carry a written authority from the organisation promoting the collection (which may be the charity or a specialist promoter). Do not be afraid to ask to see a collector's authority, and be very wary of giving money to anyone who cannot produce such a document.

---

[10] *1991 Report of the charity commissioners for England and Wales.* 1992. London, HMSO.
[11] *Charities: a framework for the future,* Government white paper. May 1989. London, HMSO.
[12] Charities Aid Foundation (CAF). 1992. *Individual giving and volunteering in Britain.* 5th edn. Tonbridge, CAF.

At present, there is no simple way of checking the authenticity of a telephone appeal, so you would be wise to avoid giving by this means. If you want to donate, suggest that the caller sends you a letter identifying the charity and its aims and that you will post any donation you make.

Checking out the charities

You can check whether an organisation is a registered charity by consulting the Central Register of Charities kept by the Charity Commissioners. You can inspect the Register weekdays from 10am–4pm at their offices (see Useful addresses on p. 167).

The Register will tell you the charity's registration number, its address and briefly what the charity does. If an organisation is on the Register, you can treat this as confirmation that it is indeed a charity.

The Charity Commission cannot usually help if your enquiry concerns a charity that is not registered, but there are a number of bodies which may be able to provide information about both registered and non-registered charities. To know whether or not an organisation has been granted charitable status, contact the Charity Division of the Inland Revenue (see p. 167).

Your local authority (address in the phone book) will usually have details of charities operating in your local area, and may have its own register which you can inspect.

The Charities Aid Foundation (CAF) – which is itself a charity, whose general aim is to promote growth in the flow of resources to the voluntary sector – produces a directory listing details of around 12,000 charities. You may find a copy in your local reference library or you can buy a copy from CAF at the address given at the back of the book. CAF may also be able to tell you about charities in your local area.

Directories are also produced by various organisations representing voluntary groups – not just charities. These organisations may be able to put you in touch with local sources of information about the charities in your area, and give you details of charities and other groups involved in particular activities or places. Contact the Council for Voluntary Organisations or the Council for Voluntary Action (see Useful addresses).

But where does the money go?

Bear in mind that, although an organisation may be a charity, neither charitable status nor registration represents a 'seal of approval'. You may still want to satisfy yourself that any money you give will be used efficiently and as you had expected. Unfortunately, there is no easy way of checking this, but a charity's financial accounts will give you some information.

All charities (whether registered or not) must prepare annual accounts describing the financial affairs of the charity over the year; most will provide you with a copy on request (and if proposed new laws are passed they will *have* to do this). Many registered charities are required by law to provide the Charity Commission with copies of their accounts. In the past, this law has been widely ignored; in 1989, it was estimated that only 11 per cent of charities who should submit their accounts actually did so.[13] Recently, however, the situation has improved and nearly half of all registered charities submitted accounts in 1991.[14] Where accounts have been submitted to the Commission, they are available for the public to inspect. You can also glean much useful information about the 400 largest charities[15] from an annual CAF publication, *Charity Trends*, which can be found in some public libraries or bought from CAF (see Useful addresses).

A charity's accounts will give you, *inter alia*, some idea about how the charity uses the funds it raises. One area of particular concern is how much of your money actually reaches the charitable cause. Inevitably, some funds must be spent on organising and running the charity itself. Research by CAF suggests people fear that nearly half of their donations might be going to pay for administration, whereas, on average, it was felt that less than a fifth should be used up in this way.[16] Interestingly, data from *Charity Trends* show that non-charitable spending by the top 50 charities is much lower than feared and amounts to only 14 per cent of income (from all sources, not just donations from the public). This figure does hide a wide range from just over 2 per cent to over 40 per cent for individual charities.[17]

---

[13]House of Commons Public Accounts Committee, reported in the *Financial Times*, 22 March 1991.
[14]*1991 Report of the Charity Commissioners for England and Wales*. 1992. London, HMSO.
[15]'Largest' in terms of income from fund raising.
[16]CAF. 1992. *Individual giving and volunteering in Britain*. 5th edn. Tonbridge, CAF. Respondents' views for home-based charities.
[17]Figures derived from CAF. 1991. *Charity Trends*. 14th edn. Tonbridge, CAF, pp.18–19.

However, you need to take care when interpreting cost figures. A high level of costs may indeed suggest inefficiency, but equally a low level of costs may be the result of the charity spending too little on administration and management. And a charity which has as its main activity giving advice, say, rather than passing on funds may justifiably have proportionately high running costs.

CHAPTER 3

SPECIAL SCHEMES FOR GIVING TO CHARITY

GIVE MORE, PAY THE SAME

'Look, here's another appeal from the Salvation Army.' Philip passed the envelope across to his wife, Mary. 'We must give something,' she said. 'Oh, did you see this?' Mary held up a pink leaflet headed *Covenanting your £10 gift could increase its value to £13.33 at no extra cost to you.* 'It says the Chancellor will add the extra, but we'd have to keep on donating for four years – well, since we give to them regularly anyway, it seems churlish not to accept the Chancellor's offer!'

Tax benefits for charities

The great advantage to an organisation of having charitable status is that it becomes eligible for a variety of tax benefits. As long as they meet certain conditions, charities enjoy complete freedom from income tax, capital gains tax and corporation tax on their income and profits from most sources. In addition, when they receive donations, charities may be able to claim back income tax which has been paid by the giver (see below).

Whereas most businesses must pay business rates to their local authority, charities are given automatic relief against four-fifths of these rates, and the local authority can exempt them from the remaining fifth if it chooses.

Charities are not completely free from tax; they are, in the main, treated like any other business when it comes to Value Added Tax (VAT). This can be a problem, especially for charities whose activities count as exempt from VAT, since they cannot reclaim VAT paid on a wide range of items that they buy. Some things charities need – for example, equipment to be used for medical research, new building for charitable purposes, and provision of toilet facilities in buildings run by charities for charitable purposes – can be purchased VAT-free. Spending on advertising is also normally VAT-free for charities.

All in all, it has been estimated that charities receive around £800 million a year in tax concessions,[18] but suffer VAT bills of around £200 million.[19]

Advantages for donors

If you make *ad hoc* donations to charity, there is usually no tax benefit to either you or the charity. But there are several special schemes which you can use that will indirectly give you tax relief by increasing the value of your gifts to charity. If you are a higher-rate taxpayer, using these schemes will directly save you tax as well. Non-taxpayers, however, should avoid these schemes because they could end up with an unexpected bill from the Inland Revenue – so watch out, in particular, if your income varies a lot.

In general, to use the special schemes you must commit yourself to some regular pattern of giving, or be prepared to donate a fairly substantial sum. However, there is one scheme – the 'loan covenant' – that can be used even for relatively small one-off sums.

The various schemes are described in the following sections.

Deed of covenant

A deed of covenant is a legally binding written promise. You agree to pay the charity a given sum of money on a regular basis. The advantage of giving in this way is that the charity can receive more than you actually give. You can use a deed of covenant to make regular gifts of any size.

By making payments through a deed of covenant, technically you

---

[18] Budget statement, March 1991.
[19] Donoghue, H. 1990. 'Tax concessions and charities – the charities' tax reform group perspective' in *Charity Trends*. 13th edn. Tonbridge, CAF.

are transferring part of your income to the charity. As such, you are also allowed to 'transfer' the tax bill associated with that income. This means that as long as you are a taxpayer, you qualify for tax relief on the amount you give to the charity. In practice, you hand over a 'net' sum to the charity – an amount from which tax at the basic-rate (25 per cent in the 1994–95 tax year) has already been deducted. You keep the tax deducted which provides you with tax relief at the basic rate. (The lower 20 per cent rate of income tax introduced in the 1992 Budget is ignored for the purpose of covenants, even if your income is low enough for it to apply to you.)

If you are a higher-rate taxpayer, there is more tax relief due to you that you must reclaim directly from the Inland Revenue.[20] Normally, you do this after the end of the tax year by giving details of your covenant payments to charity on your tax return. The Inland Revenue will then either send you a cheque or adjust your PAYE code as appropriate.

The charity is exempt from income tax and so can claim back from the Inland Revenue the tax you have deducted, thus boosting the size of your gift.

EXAMPLE 3.1

Mary thinks she would like the Salvation Army to receive £100 a year through a deed of covenant. She is a basic-rate taxpayer, so she would agree to hand over £75 each year (£100 less £25 tax at the basic rate of 25 per cent). The charity would reclaim £25 from the Inland Revenue bringing the total it received up to £100.

But Philip suggests that he should make the donations because he's a higher-rate (40 per cent) taxpayer and would qualify for more tax relief than Mary. Like Mary, he would hand over £75 a year to the charity. The Salvation Army would reclaim £25 from the Inland Revenue bringing the total the charity received to £100. Philip would then contact his tax office and be able to reclaim a further £15 (15 per cent of £100) in tax relief. So it would cost Philip just £60 to give the charity £100. His extra tax relief is given to him through his pay by adjusting his PAYE code.

---

[20]But if a charity uses part of a covenanted gift for non-charitable purposes (other than meeting reasonable administration costs), higher-rate tax relief may be reduced or even withdrawn completely.

To qualify for special tax treatment, you must intend to make covenanted payments to the charity for at least four years. Nevertheless, although strictly speaking the covenant is legally binding, it is unlikely that a charity would insist that you keep up the payments if, say, you fell on hard times.

Often a charitable covenant will specify that payments are to be made for four years or until some later event, such as giving up membership of the charity. In the past, such a covenant ceased to be effective at the end of four years and the charity concerned would have to ask you to renew your covenant. But, since 1992, covenants with this type of wording automatically continue to be valid after the first four years without the need for renewal.

To satisfy the tax rules, the wording of a deed of covenant must be very precise. Fortunately, you do not need to worry about this, because nearly all charities will gladly provide you with a suitable covenant form (an example is shown below). You just need to add the relevant details and your signature. In England, Wales and Northern Ireland, you will need someone to witness your signature. (In Scotland, you will need either two witnesses or none at all, but where you do not have a witness you must write 'Adopted as holograph' above your signature.)

EXAMPLE OF A COVENANT TO CHARITY

DEED OF COVENANT

I _____ (*your name*) of _____ (*your address*) undertake to pay _____ (*name of charity*) each year for four years (or during my lifetime if shorter) the sum that will after deduction of income tax at the basic rate be £_____ (*amount you want to give*) from _____ (*date of first payment*).

Signed and delivered by _____ (*your signature*)
Date _____ (*date you sign the covenant*)

Witness's signature _____
Witness's address _____

The example of a covenant (opposite) is a 'net covenant': that is, you agree to hand over a fixed sum of money to the charity each year. If the basic tax rate changed, you would still hand over the same amount, but the charity would reclaim a changed amount of tax. More rarely, you might use a 'gross covenant' to make charitable gifts; with this, you agree to give the charity a fixed *before-tax* sum. If the basic tax rate changes, the amount you hand over to the charity also changes — but so does the amount of tax relief the charity re-claims, so the charity continues to receive the same total (gross) sum.

If you are interested in giving by covenant, there are a few points to watch out for, as follows:

- A covenant cannot be backdated, so make sure that the first payment under it falls due *after* the covenant has been signed.
- If you are a non-taxpayer in any year when a payment is made under the covenant, the charity will still be able to claim tax relief, but the Inland Revenue will then ask you to hand over a sum equal to the tax relief given. So, if you are a non-taxpayer or expect to become one during the course of the covenant's life, do not make gifts to charity in this way.
- A covenant is not normally valid if you receive something in return for making the payments.

This last point can be a problem for charities which offer various benefits to subscribing members: for example, magazines, free use of premises, or free entry to otherwise commercial events. As the law stands, a covenant can be used to pay the subscription only if any benefits to the members are minimal; in other cases, the covenant would not be valid and the special tax treatment would not apply. There is an exception: a covenant is a valid way of paying the subscription to a charity which gives free or reduced-rate admission to properties preserved for the public benefit or places where wildlife is conserved for the public benefit. This means, for example, that members of the National Trust can pay their subscription by covenant.

There are no hard-and-fast figures showing how much money is raised for charities through covenants, but estimates based on data for 1985–86 suggest that £179 million (including tax relief) was given to charity by covenant in that year.[21]

[21]Jones, A. and Posnett, J. 1990. 'Giving by covenant in the UK'. In *Charity Trends*. 13th edn. Tonbridge, CAF. (Their analysis was based on the Inland Revenue *Survey of personal incomes* for 1985–86.)

If you are an employee and a higher-rate taxpayer and you want to give no more than £75 a month to charity, consider 'Payroll Giving' (see p. 33) instead of using a covenant (if your employer operates a scheme). With Payroll Giving, you get all the tax relief due to you at the time you make your gift rather than having to wait for the higher-rate relief.

Loan covenant

A loan covenant (also called a 'deposited covenant' or 'deposited deed') is a way of donating a lump sum to a charity but still benefiting from the tax advantages of a covenant. You agree to give money to a charity under a normal deed of covenant lasting, say, four years. But, at the same time, you make an interest-free loan to the charity which is to be repaid in four yearly instalments. The loan repayments are used to make the gifts under the covenant. As each covenant payment is made, the charity can claim back tax in the normal way – and you can claim higher-rate tax relief on the covenant payments in any year in which you are a higher-rate taxpayer.

EXAMPLE 3.2

Harold likes to support charities when he can afford to. He works for himself and his income is a bit erratic, so he has never liked the idea of committing himself to regular donations. But, at present, work is going well, and he has decided to make a gift of £200 to the London Association for the Blind, a national charity helping blind and partially sighted people. If he pays the £200 using a loan covenant, the charity will actually receive £266.67 in total. The scheme works as shown in the Table (Harold is definitely expected to earn enough to be a basic-rate taxpayer throughout the next four years). If Harold could give just £50 more, he could use the Gift Aid scheme instead (see opposite).

Year	1991–92	1992–93	1993–94	1994–95
Harold makes a loan to the charity	£200			
Charity repays the loan	£50	£50	£50	£50
Payments under the deed of covenant (financed by the loan repayments)	£50	£50	£50	£50
Basic-rate tax relief reclaimed by the charity on the covenant payments[1]	£16.67	£16.67	£16.67	£16.67
Total received by the charity	£66.67	£66.67	£66.67	£66.67

[1]Assuming basic-rate tax continues to be 25 per cent.

Loan covenants can be used to make lump sum gifts of any size, but the administration costs involved mean that gifts below, say, £100 are not worthwhile via this route. And bear in mind that tax relief for the charity and for higher-rate taxpayers is spread over the lifetime of the covenant. If you want to give £250 or more you should instead choose the 'Gift Aid' scheme (see below); with this scheme tax relief is given straight away.

Gift Aid

You can use Gift Aid to make fairly large lump-sum gifts to charity. The scheme is rather similar to using a covenant in that you hand over a sum which is deemed to be net of basic-rate income tax. (As with covenants, the lower 20 per cent rate is ignored.) The charity can then reclaim the tax deducted. If you are a higher-rate taxpayer, you can claim higher-rate tax relief direct from your tax office. Usually, you will do this after the end of the tax year in which you make the gift by filling in the appropriate section of your tax return.

To use Gift Aid, the net sum you give must be £250 or more for payments made after 16 March 1993. (The limit was £400 before that date and £600 before 1 July 1992.) If you make a gift jointly with other people – your husband or wife, say, or work colleagues – you can still use Gift Aid as long as your share of the gift is £250 or more. There is no upper limit on the amount you can donate.

EXAMPLE 3.3

Following the death of close friend from cancer, Philip gave £750 to the Imperial Cancer Research Fund last year using the Gift Aid scheme. The charity was able to reclaim basic-rate tax of £250 bringing the total it received to £1,000. Philip reclaimed higher-rate relief of £150 (15 per cent of £1,000) from his tax office. This means that Philip paid just £600 to make a gift of £1,000 to the charity.

There are several points to watch out for when considering using the Gift Aid scheme, as follows:

- If you are a non-taxpayer, the charity will still be able to claim tax relief but the Inland Revenue will ask you for a sum equal to the amount of relief given.
- You cannot combine Gift Aid with any of the other tax-advantageous ways of giving to charity. So, for example, you cannot use a Gift Aid donation to finance a series of covenant payments.
- The tax advantages will be withdrawn if you (or anyone connected with you, such as family or close business associates) receive anything more than a purely token benefit in return for the donation. This means that, for example, you cannot use Gift Aid to pay school fees, or to buy a season ticket for the opera.

When you hand over your gift, you must also give the charity a completed **Form R190(SD)** which certifies that your payment is eligible for the scheme. The charity can provide you with this form. If you do not complete an R190(SD), the charity will not be able to claim tax relief.

The Gift Aid scheme has been running since 1 October 1990 and raised nearly £470 million in net gifts (£630 million including tax relief) in the period to June 1993.[22] (These figures include gifts made by companies as well as individuals.)

---

[22]Inland Revenue press release, 15 September 1993.

Payroll Giving schemes

Payroll Giving (also called 'Payroll Deduction' and often referred to as 'Give-As-You-Earn') is a method of making regular gifts to charity out of your pay-packet. It is open only to employees, and only to those whose employer operates a Payroll Giving scheme. You can give any amount up to a maximum of £900 in total during the tax year (£75 a month). Prior to 6 April 1993 the limit was £600.

The scheme works like this. Your employer sets up an arrangement with an agency charity. You then tell your employer how much you want to give each pay day and to which charity or charities. The employer deducts the specified amount from your pay and hands it over to the agency charity which arranges for the money to be transferred to the charities you picked. (The agency may make a charge – for example, five per cent of the donations it handles – to cover its own running costs, but some agency charities charge nothing.) Your donation is deducted from your pay before tax (but not National Insurance) is worked out, so you automatically get full income tax relief.

EXAMPLE 3.4

Mary earns £640 a month, before tax, working in the local branch of a national building society. The society operates a Payroll Giving scheme through which Mary gives £10 a month each to Help the Aged and Dr Barnardo's. Normally, Mary would pay £75.73 a month in income tax (during the 1994-95 tax year), but after deducting the Payroll Giving from her pay, the tax bill is reduced to £70.73 a month. In other words, she gets tax relief of £5, which reduces the cost to her of the £20 she gives to charity to just £15.

If your employer operates a Payroll Giving scheme, he can provide you with details and an application form.

You do not have to keep up your donations for any minimum period of time. You stop making them whenever you like simply by informing your employer of your wishes.

Payroll Giving cannot be used in combination with any of the other tax-advantageous ways of giving to charity. So, for example, you cannot make gifts under a deed of covenant through a Payroll Giving scheme.

Payroll Giving was introduced in April 1987. After a slow start, use of these schemes has been increasing steadily. By the year to April 1991, Payroll Giving schemes covered some 278,000 employees who gave around £9.3 million to charity in this way, and 3,900 employers operated these schemes.[23]

---

[23]CAF. 1991. *Charity Trends*. 14th edn. Tonbridge, CAF.

CHAPTER 4

Other ways of giving to charity

PAY NOW, GIVE LATER

Mary stood chatting to her neighbour, Jack, about charity appeals. 'I set aside a certain amount for charities,' he said, 'but I bide my time about which charities I give to. You see, I have a special charity account – I pay money in, the account claims a bit extra from the taxman, and I have a sort of – well – a cheque book. When I want to donate to a cause, I simply write out a cheque drawn on my account.'

'What a splendid idea,' marvelled Mary. 'Who runs this charity account?'

Apart from the special schemes outlined in the previous chapter, there are a number of other ways of giving to charity that can give either you or the charity some tax advantage. Some are sophisticated schemes, really only suitable if you have a large sum to give. Others are widely useful and can provide a way round some of the inconveniences of the special schemes described in Chapter 3.

There is also one popular method of giving which, though not tax-efficient, does enable the charity to receive more than you give. The various methods are described below.

Giving things rather than cash

You do not have to give just cash as a charitable donation. You could instead give something you own: for example, land, a car, furniture, and so on. As described in Part 2, normally, you might have to pay capital gains tax (CGT) and even inheritance tax (IHT) when you give something away. But gifts to charities are generally completely free of these taxes.

For the exemption from IHT to apply, you must relinquish all your rights to whatever it is that you are giving. For example, there might well be a tax bill if you gave the freehold of your home to a charity but continued to live there. For more details about the way CGT and IHT work, see Chapters 5–7.

Charitable bequests

If you leave money or assets to charity in your will, your estate pays no IHT on the gift. (Your estate is all your possessions less any debts at the time of death.)

A bequest to charity can also save IHT in a second way, because the value of your estate is reduced by the amount of your gift to charity. This can mean less IHT on the estate as a whole. Bear in mind, though, that making a bequest to charity cuts down the amount of the estate left for your survivors to inherit, so you should not use this as a tax-saving method unless you intended to make philanthropic gifts anyway.

All gifts from your estate when you die – whether to charity or to other organisations or to people – are free of CGT.

See Part 3 for more information about gifts made at the time of death.

CAF Charity Account

The Charities Aid Foundation (CAF) is a charity whose aim is to promote charities generally and give them support and assistance. One of the services it runs is the CAF Charity Account. This is a little like a bank account but its sole purpose is for making gifts to charity. The advantages of the Account are that the money you give is increased by tax relief, and you have a convenient, flexible way of giving to a wide range of charities. The Account works as follows.

You pay money into your Charity Account using a deed of covenant, Gift Aid, or the CAF Payroll Giving scheme called 'Give-

As-You-Earn' (see Chapter 3). Because CAF is itself a charity, it is able to claim tax relief on the money you pay in using covenants or Gift Aid and it adds this to your Account. With Payroll Giving you qualify for tax relief directly as normal. When you want to make a gift to a charity, you instruct CAF to transfer money from your Account to the charity. You can do this in several ways, as follows:

- CAF provides you with a 'cheque book' of vouchers. You fill in a voucher and give it to the charity which is to receive your gift. The charity sends the voucher to CAF which then transfers the money as you have instructed.
- You can ask CAF to make regular payments to a particular charity using a standing order system.
- You can ask CAF to make a single payment to a particular charity.
- You can leave instructions with CAF about how the money in the account is to be donated in the event of your death.

CAF makes a charge for running the Account: three per cent of each payment made into the Account under a deed of covenant, and three per cent of each payment made into the Account under Gift Aid. The charges are based on the *gross* amount of your payment: for example, if you make a net Gift Aid payment of £750, this would have a gross value (after adding back tax relief) of £1,000. CAF would deduct three per cent of £1,000: that is, £30. On covenants of £10,000 or more, charges are reduced. With both covenanted and Gift Aid payments, there is a maximum charge of £575 a year. If you make payments into the Account using Give-As-You-Earn, there is no separate charge for running the Charity Account, but there is a charge for using the Give-As-You-Earn scheme of five per cent of each payment – sometimes your employer will pay this for you.[24]

EXAMPLE 4.1

Jack, puts money into his CAF Charity Account using a deed of covenant (see p. 26). Under the deed, he pays an after-tax amount of £150 a year into the Account. When each payment is made, CAF reclaims basic-rate tax relief of £50 bringing the total which is paid into the Account each year to £200. (Jack is a basic-rate taxpayer, so he cannot directly reclaim any tax himself.)

[24]Charges as at July 1992.

CAF deducts a charge of £6 a year, leaving £194. Out of this, Jack has a standing order to pay £50 a year to the Royal National Institute for the Deaf. He uses his 'cheque book' to make other donations: for example, last year, he made out 'cheques' to Childline, Help the Aged and the RSPCA.

The normal rules which apply to covenants, Gift Aid and Payroll Giving apply when you are using the CAF Charity Account. For example, if you pay into the Account using Gift Aid, you cannot use it to pay subscriptions for membership of charitable bodies. But, if you pay into the Account using a covenant, you can use it to pay your subscription to a few organisations, such as The National Trust (see p. 29). The CAF Charity Account is not suitable for non-taxpayers who would receive a bill from the Inland Revenue for the tax relief paid over to CAF under covenants or Gift Aid.

For details about the Charity Account, contact CAF at the address at the back of the book.

Discretionary trusts

A trust is a special legal arrangement where money, shares, or other property are held for the benefit of others. Trustees have the duty of seeing that the property in the trust and any income and gains from it (which together make up the 'trust fund') are used as set out in the trust deed and rules. With a 'discretionary trust', the trustees are given the power to decide how the trust fund is used (within any constraints imposed by the trust rules).

Special tax rules apply to trusts (see Chapter 9), but it is worth noting here that gifts to charity from a discretionary trust can be very tax-efficient. The charity will be able to reclaim all the income tax – usually at 35 per cent rather than just the basic rate – that the trust has paid on the income it gives. If the trust makes a gift to charity of capital, there will be no CGT or IHT to pay on it.

Charitable trusts

Many charities are organised as 'charitable trusts': that is, trustees hold money for the benefit of others and use or distribute it according to the rules set out in the trust deed and rules, but the trust also qualifies for special tax treatment because it meets the requirements for charitable status (see p. 21). It is not just organisations that can use charitable trusts; you can, in effect, set up your own charity to give funds to other charities. This would be worth doing if:

- you wanted to give a large sum to charity or to give regular sizeable amounts, and
- you wanted to split the donation between several charities (especially where each gift is below £250 and so would not qualify for tax relief through Gift Aid) and/or
- you had not yet decided which charities to give some or all of the money to.

Setting up your own charitable trust is fairly complex and costly and worth doing only if you intend to give large amounts to charity. It can be used both to make gifts in your lifetime and gifts in your will. In either case, you should seek advice from a solicitor or from the Charities Aid Foundation (CAF) (see p. 36).

To use a charitable trust to make lifetime gifts, you would set up a trust – usually a discretionary trust (see Chapter 9 for more about these) – often with yourself as one of the trustees. Once the trust deed has been drawn up (but before it is completed), you need to send it to the Charity Commission, which, in consultation with the Inland Revenue, will decide whether the trust will qualify as a charity. As long as it will, you can go ahead and set up the trust, and it will be exempt from most taxes in the same way as a normal charity (see pp. 25–26). This means that you will be able to make tax-efficient donations into the trust to be passed on to the charities you choose. For example, you could covenant to pay a given sum to the trust for a period of four years or more, or you could donate a lump sum of £250 or more under the Gift Aid scheme. The trust would be able to claim back tax on the payments in the same way as a normal charity. (But when the trust itself makes payments to a charity, it cannot use a special scheme, such as a deed of covenant or Gift Aid – you cannot get tax relief twice!)

EXAMPLE 4.2

Daisy married a wealthy landowner but was widowed many years ago. Daisy's 'good causes' are famous in her family. One of her projects is a charitable trust to which she pays £10,000 a year under a deed of covenant. The trust claims basic-rate tax of £3,333 bringing the total it receives each year to £13,333. Daisy claims higher-rate tax relief of nearly £2,000, so she can give £13,333 at a cost to herself of just £8,000.

The trust is a discretionary trust. Daisy is a trustee and largely decides how the trust money will be used. The trust aims to help people who are in sudden and urgent need: for example, in 1993, it paid £5,000 to charities providing famine relief in North Africa, £1,500 to help Bosnian refugees, and £1,500 to a local charity to help families in financial distress following the closure of a major employer in the area. If the trust does not pay out the full £13,333 in any year, the remainder is invested to be used for charitable causes in future years.

You can set up a charitable trust in your will to receive a bequest. The bequest would reduce the size of your estate for tax purposes and could mean there is less IHT to be paid (see Part 3). The deed and rules of the charitable trust would specify how the bequest is to be used: for example, you might want the capital to remain invested while the income from it is donated to charity, or you might want the trustees to decide to which charities the capital and/or income are to be given. You can even set up a 'temporary charitable trust' where the trust funds are used for charitable purposes for a specified period but then revert to a non-charitable use: for example, you might direct that income be donated to charity until your grandchildren come of age when the trust money is to be split between them. When a temporary charitable trust stops being used for charitable purposes, there will be an income tax bill and possibly a CGT bill. The rules are complex, so seek professional advice before setting up this type of trust.

There is always a risk that a trust set up under a will might not be recognised by the authorities as charitable even though it was your intention that it should be. To avoid this risk, you could set up the trust during your lifetime, paying just a small amount into it now; this gives you the chance to alter the trust if the Inland Revenue is not satisfied that it meets the requirements for a charity. Once charitable status has been secured, you can safely make a bequest to the trust in your will.

Gifts from businesses

If you run your own company or you are self-employed, there are a number of tax-efficient ways in which you can give to charity. Similarly, a club which is set up as a limited company can use the methods outlined in this section.

Ideally, you would be able to treat a gift to charity as an allowable business expense since this would reduce your profits and thus tax on them. But normal business rules apply and your gift would have to be made 'wholly and exclusively for the purposes of trade' in order to be allowable. Most charitable gifts just do not fit the bill. However, there are a number of quirks and concessions in the tax rules which mean that you should be able to treat the following sorts of gifts to charities as an allowable expense:

- Small gifts of money, or gifts in kind, to support a local charity provided the gift has a business purpose – for example, donations to a local charity that benefits your employees in some way.
- Sponsorship of a charity event as long as it provides you with advertising.
- All the costs of employing someone, even though seconded temporarily to work for a charity rather than working for you.

Most business gifts to charity are *not* allowable expenses, but businesses can use both deeds of covenant (see p. 26) and Gift Aid (see p. 31) to make gifts in much the same way as an individual. The business makes a gift from which basic-rate income tax has been deducted. The charity reclaims the tax from the Inland Revenue, thus boosting the size of the gift. If you are self-employed, you simply keep the tax you have deducted from the gift as long as you are liable for at least that much tax yourself. A company must pay the tax it has deducted from the gift over to the Inland Revenue, but can then deduct the gross amount of the gift from its taxable profits and thus get relief from corporation tax.

It is worth noting that, under a covenant, you do not have to specify that each payment you make will be a particular sum of money. You could instead covenant, say, a specified proportion of your annual profits.

EXAMPLE 4.3

Jack is the treasurer of a car racing club which meets regularly during the summer months. At the meetings, both members and spectators are charged an entrance fee and there are other takings for refreshments. The club always gives the income from these meetings, after deducting costs, to a charity.

The club is set up as a limited company. In order to take advantage of the tax relief available on charitable giving, it decides to covenant the profits from each season's race meetings to Cancer and Leukaemia in Childhood Trust (CLIC). Despite the fact that the profits vary and cannot be known at the time the covenant is drawn up, this is a valid form of covenant.

For the self-employed and those working for 'close companies' (i.e. companies controlled by their directors or by five or fewer participants, as are many family companies) there used to be no simple means of making small, one-off gifts to charity tax-efficiently (apart from using a 'loan covenant' – see p. 30), but with the reduction of the Gift Aid limit to £250 this is no longer a problem. And companies which are not 'close' can give away any amount up to three per cent of the dividends paid out on the ordinary shares. As with covenants and Gift Aid, the company gives an amount that is net of basic-rate income tax and the charity claims tax relief. The company pays the tax it has deducted from the gift to the Inland Revenue, but can deduct the gross amount of the gift from its taxable profits and thus get relief against corporation tax.

Affinity cards

A number of charities and credit card companies have combined forces to issue affinity cards. These are just normal credit cards, but the card company promises to make donations to charity linked to your use of the credit card. For example, NatWest makes donations to the World Wide Fund for Nature (WWF) through the NatWest WWF Card – a VISA card. When you open the account, NatWest donates £6 to WWF, and for every £100 you spend using the card, NatWest donates a further 20 pence to WWF. Other examples of credit card/charity link-ups include the Canine Defence League and Royal Bank of Scotland (Mastercard), Imperial Cancer Research and Leeds Permanent Building Society (VISA), The National Trust and Midland Bank (VISA), Oxfam and Girobank (VISA), Royal Society for the Protection of Birds and Co-op Bank (VISA), and Save the Children and TSB (VISA).

The credit card company can use an affinity card scheme to make tax-efficient donations to charity, but it is, of course, a marketing exercise for the company, attracting customers and helping to project a caring image. If you use a credit card anyway, an affinity card is a way in which you can play an indirect role in giving to charity, but compare interest rates and other terms with standard credit cards before you commit yourself. It may be better to stick with your existing credit card and arrange to make your donations direct to charity. If you do not normally use a credit card, you should be wary of taking out an affinity card: do not run up debts that you cannot afford.

SUMMARY OF GIFTS TO CHARITY

Method of giving	Can you give a single lump sum?	Suitable for 'small' (£250 or less) gifts?	Can a payment be split into gifts for several charities?
Covenant	No	Yes	No
Loan covenant	Yes	Yes[25]	No
Gift Aid	Yes	No	No
Payroll Giving	No	Yes	Yes
Give assets	Yes	Yes	No
Charitable bequest	Yes	Yes	Maybe
CAF charity account – by covenant	No	Yes	Yes
CAF charity account – by Gift Aid	Yes	No	Yes
CAF charity account – by Payroll Giving	No	Yes	Yes
Discretionary trust	Yes	No[26]	Yes
Charitable trust	Yes	No[26]	Yes

[25] But administration costs mean that gifts under £100 or so would not normally be worthwhile using this method.
[26] Small gifts are technically possible but unsuitable, given the cost and administration involved in setting up the trust.

PART 2

LIFETIME GIFTS TO FAMILY AND FRIENDS

CHAPTER 5

TAX-FREE GIFTS

THE CHOICE OF GIFT MATTERS

'Sylvia,' Jeffrey turned solemnly to his wife, 'I think we should give Tom a helping hand to buy a home now that he's settling down.'

'I couldn't agree more. But to be fair to the girls, we ought to set aside some money to help them later on too,' replied Sylvia.

'It doesn't have to be money of course – they might like to have one or two of the paintings. I wonder if it makes a tax difference? I do believe that we could give Tom a bit of money as a wedding present without running into tax problems . . .'

There are two main taxes that you need to be aware of when making a gift to someone: capital gains tax (CGT) and inheritance tax (IHT). Some gifts can also affect your income tax position – an aspect which can be to your advantage as long as you arrange the gift in a suitable way (see Chapter 8). This chapter looks at gifts you can make during your lifetime that are either free of CGT, free of IHT, or completely free of both taxes. Subsequent chapters look at gifts which may be taxable.

Capital gains tax

When you give someone something that you own, you are treated for tax purposes as making a 'disposal' of an 'asset'. An 'asset' is simply something which you own. 'Disposal' means ceasing to own the asset, however this comes about – the tax position when you give away an asset is essentially the same as if you had sold it.

If an asset's value at the time you give it away is greater than its value at the time you first started to own it, there *could* be a CGT bill. But don't panic! Often you won't have to pay any CGT, because:

- some assets are outside the scope of CGT
- gains from some transactions are always tax-free.

The scope of capital gains tax

CGT is a tax on the disposal of *assets*. 'Assets' covers virtually all types of property: land, buildings, stocks and shares, paintings, furniture, patents and copyrights, debts owed to you, and so on. 'Assets', for CGT purposes, does not include sterling currency – so a gift of money cannot result in a CGT bill. By an interesting quirk of the law, sovereigns minted after 1837 still count as sterling currency and are thus outside the CGT net.

Certain other assets are specifically exempt from CGT. These are looked at in the following sections.

'Chattels'
These are tangible, movable assets – basically your personal possessions and household goods. An item in this category is exempt from CGT provided it has a predicted useful life of 50 years or less and you have not used it in a business.

For chattels with an expected life of more than 50 years, any gain is exempt if the value of the item at the time you dispose of it is no more than £6,000. If a chattel's value is more than £6,000, any gain can be worked out in a special way which may reduce the CGT bill (see Example 6.2 on p. 61). There are rules to prevent you reducing the CGT payable by splitting up a set – for example, a set of chairs – and then giving all the parts of the set to the same person.

Your home
There is no CGT to pay when you dispose of part or all of your only, or main, home. This exemption includes your garden up to a reasonable size (usually half a hectare – just over an acre – but it can be more if the style and size of house warrants a larger garden).

If you have more than one house, you will have to nominate one as your main home for CGT purposes (though this does not have to be the one you generally live in). A husband and wife who live together can have only one main home between them. (But if one of them counts as non-resident for a tax year, husband and wife can each have a main home for CGT purposes.)

You may lose part of the exemption if part of your home was set aside exclusively for business. There may also be a CGT bill when you dispose of your home, if you have lived away for long periods.

EXAMPLE 5.1

Daisy has decided that Hadley Hall where she has lived since her marriage is now too large for her needs. She plans to give the Hall to her only son, Albert, and buy a cottage nearby. When Daisy inherited the Hall on her husband's death it was worth £150,000. It is now worth twice that, but there will be no CGT bill because:

- the Hall is Daisy's only home, and
- although the garden runs to over two acres, the Inland Revenue has agreed that this is in keeping with the house.

However, Daisy does need to consider the IHT position (see Chapter 7).

Motor vehicles

There is no CGT on gains from selling or giving away a private car (including vintage or classic cars), a motorbike, or other private motor vehicle. This exemption can also apply to a vehicle used for business provided it was 'commonly used as a private vehicle'.

Foreign currency

There is no CGT on gains from buying and selling foreign money which you have obtained for your own use – for a holiday abroad, say, or for buying or running a holiday home abroad, or for use during a business trip.

Some investments

Gains on some investments are completely free from CGT: for example, National Savings investments, Premium Bonds, British Government stocks (gilts), many corporate bonds, and shares held through a Personal Equity Plan (PEP). Provided certain conditions are met, gains on shares bought through a Business Expansion Scheme (BES) are also CGT-free. Similarly, gains on investments bought through the new Enterprise Investment Schemes, announced in the November 1993 Budget, are to be free of CGT.

Insurance policies

Payment from a policy, whether on maturity, early surrender, or even through selling the policy to someone else, is usually exempt from CGT. The exemption does not apply, however, if you bought the policy from someone else: for example, through an auction.

Tax-free transactions

Some *transactions* are also exempt from CGT. This means that the following types of gift are free of CGT.

Gifts between husband and wife

Gifts between husband and wife are free of CGT provided the couple are living together.

Gifts to charities and certain other bodies

Donations and gifts to charity, and to various other institutions, including many museums and art galleries, local authorities, government departments and universities, are CGT-free.

Gifts for the public benefit

Gifts of 'eligible property' to any non-profit body approved by the government are outside the CGT net. 'Eligible property' includes land or buildings of outstanding historic or aesthetic interest, and property to be used as a source of income for the upkeep of such land or buildings. It also covers items such as books, pictures, scientific collections and so on which are judged to be of national interest.

Gifts on death

When you die, you are deemed to make a gift of all you then own to your heirs, but whatever, and however much, you leave, it is always free of CGT.

Inheritance tax

IHT is a tax on the 'transfer of value' from one person to another. 'Transfer of value' means a gift (or other transaction) which reduces the value of the possessions (the 'estate') owned by the person making the transfer. In theory, it could apply to any gift you make but, as with CGT, there are various exemptions and adjustments. This means that on most lifetime gifts there is no IHT to pay, because:

- various types of gift are always free of IHT
- some gifts, called 'potentially exempt transers', are free of tax, provided the giver lives on for seven years after making the gift.

Gifts which are always free of IHT

The scope of IHT is, on the face of it, wider than that of CGT because IHT covers all assets – including money, as well as houses, land, pictures, furniture, and so on. But gifts made in certain circumstances or between certain people or bodies are free of IHT. This applies to the following gifts, whether you make them during your lifetime or as bequests in your will (see Chapter 11).

Gifts between husband and wife

Gifts between husband and wife up to any amount are tax-free as long as the couple are not divorced. Even a husband and wife who are separated benefit from this exemption. If the husband or wife receiving the gift is not 'domiciled' in the United Kingdom, the exemption is limited to a total of £55,000. (Your place of 'domicile' is, broadly, where you make your permanent home and intend to end your days.)

Gifts to charities and other bodies

This exemption from IHT is similar to the equivalent one for CGT (see p. 52). It covers outright donations and gifts of any amount to UK charities, national museums and art galleries, universities, local authorities, government departments, and a number of other bodies.

Gifts for the public benefit

Again this is similar to the associated CGT exemption (see p. 52). Gifts of land, buildings, works of art, and so on, of outstanding national interest are free of IHT if given to a suitable non-profit-making body that has been approved by the government.

Gifts to political parties

A gift to a political party is exempt from IHT, provided the party has at least two MPs or polled at least 150,000 votes at the most recent general election.

Housing Associations

Gifts of land to a Registered Housing Association are exempt.

Lifetime gifts which are free of IHT

The following gifts are free of IHT only when they are made during your lifetime (i.e. not in your will).

Normal expenditure out of income

If you can show that a gift you are making is one of a regular pattern of similar gifts and that you are making it out of your income (rather than from your savings or other capital), the gift will be exempt from IHT.

Gifts made under a legally binding agreement, such as a deed of covenant, will usually be treated as regular gifts. So too will premiums you pay for an insurance policy that is for the benefit of someone else: for example, a policy on your life which would pay out to your children in the event of your death. If the gifts are not made under any formal agreement but you intend that they will be regular gifts, they can still qualify for the exemption. The first gift or two might not be treated as exempt at the time you make it but, once a regular pattern has been established, they can be reassessed as tax-exempt.

The gifts must be made out of your income, so you need to be able to show that you have enough income left to meet your day-to-day living expenses. The income can be from any source – a job, interest from investments, and so on. But bear in mind that the capital element of a 'purchased life annuity' (see p. 164) is not income, nor are withdrawals from 'single premium life insurance bonds' (see p. 164).

Normally, the gifts would be cash. If you make gifts which are not cash you will have to be able to prove that the things you are giving were bought out of your income.

Gifts for the maintenance of your family

Money or things which you give to provide housing, food, education, or some other form of maintenance, for your husband or wife, ex-husband or ex-wife, children or a dependent relative are outside the IHT net.

As far as husband and wife are concerned, the normal exemption for gifts between married couples (see p. 53) would usually apply rather than this exemption. But if either husband or wife are 'domiciled' (see p. 53) abroad, this exemption could be useful. This exemption will usually cover maintenance agreements made as a result of a marriage breakdown.

The definition of children is very wide covering stepchildren, illegitimate children, and adopted children, but it does not extend to grandchildren. Usually a child is considered to be adult when they reach the age of 18 but, if they go on to full-time education or training after that age, the IHT exemption can carry on.

Yearly tax-free exemption

Every tax year, you can make up to £3,000 of gifts without them counting in any way for IHT purposes. This exemption is in addition to the other exemptions, so a gift which qualifies for some other exemption does not count towards the £3,000 annual limit.

If you do not use up the full exemption one year, you can carry it forward to the next year – but not to any subsequent year. This means that, if you used none of last year's exemption, you could make up to £6,000 worth of gifts this year that qualify for the exemption. Gifts always use up the exemption for the tax year in which they are made first *before* using up any carried-foward exemption.

EXAMPLE 5.2

Albert is not altogether pleased at being given Hadley Hall by Daisy (see p. 51). She has paid little attention to the house in the last 20 years and now the roof needs reslating and all the exterior woodwork is in bad need of a new coat of paint. After several heated discussions, Daisy finally agrees to give Albert £5,000 to pay for the work. Albert persuades Daisy to pay the money to a company which he runs rather than direct to him.

A gift from a person to a company would usually be taxable under the IHT rules. But, in this case, there is no IHT to pay because Daisy has not used her annual exemption for either this year or last year. The gift to Albert uses up the full £3,000 exemption available for this year and £2,000 of the exemption carried forward from last year. There remains £1,000 of last year's exemption which can be set against any other chargeable gifts made this year, but it cannot be carried forward any further.

Small gifts

You can make as many gifts as you like of up to £250 to each person, and these will be exempt. You cannot combine the small gift exemption with another exemption to give more than £250 to *one* person, but you can, say, give £3,000 to one recipient and gifts of £250 to any number of *other* people.

This exemption will generally cover birthday and Christmas presents, and any other small gifts you make during the year.

Wedding gifts

As a parent, you can give up to £5,000 to the happy couple free of IHT. A grandparent (or other ancestor) can give up to £2,500. Anyone else can give up to £1,000. The bride and groom can give up to £2,500 to each other, but this limit will not be relevant if both are 'domiciled' (see p. 53) in the United Kingdom, since the exemption for married couples (see above) will apply.

The exemptions apply to each giver: for example, assuming both bride's and groom's mothers and fathers were living, the couple could receive a maximum of £20,000 from their parents.

The exemptions under this section can also apply to a marriage settlement which aims to benefit the bride or groom, their children, or the husbands or wives of their children.

Potentially exempt transfers

A potentially exempt transfer (PET) is a gift from a person either to another person or to certain types of trust (see Chapter 9) that is not covered by some other IHT exemption. As long as the person making the gift survives for seven years after the date of the gift, there is IHT to pay. If the giver dies within seven years, there may be an IHT bill. PETs are looked at in detail in Chapter 7.

EXAMPLE 5.3

Daisy's gift of Hadley Hall to Albert is valued at £300,000. Despite the substantial value of the gift, there is no IHT to pay at the time of the gift, because it counts as a potentially exempt transfer (PET). As long as Daisy survives for seven years, there will be no IHT at all. But if she does die within that time, the gift will be reassessed and tax may then be due, depending on the value of the Hall at the time of the original gift (i.e. £300,000), Daisy's overall IHT position at that time and IHT rates at the time of death (see pp. 79–81).

Combining CGT and IHT exemptions

Some types of gift are specifically exempt from both CGT and IHT: for example, gifts to charities, museums, and so on, and gifts for the public benefit. Other gifts will be completely tax-free as long as they fall within an IHT exemption *and* you give cash or other assets which are not liable for CGT. Chapters 6 and 7 describe other situations in which either CGT or IHT may not be payable. You can make use of the exemptions in these situations too, to ensure that your gifts are free of both taxes.

EXAMPLE 5.4

Jeffrey gives his son, Tom, £4,000 in cash as a wedding gift to help him and his new wife buy a home of their own. There is no CGT on a gift of cash and no IHT on a wedding gift of this size.

Jeffrey also wants to give his youngest daughter, Ruth, a gift of similar value. She decides she would like to have a watercolour – a family heirloom – which is valued at £4,500. This counts as a 'chattel' (see p. 50) and, since its value is less than £6,000, there is no CGT liability. The gift is a PET under the IHT rules, and so, since Jeffrey is expected to live a good many years longer, the gift is likely to be completely free of IHT.

CHAPTER 6

CAPITAL GAINS TAX ON LIFETIME GIFTS

AND STILL NO TAX TO PAY

'Congratulations!' Frederick raised his glass and drank his son's health. 'And now you are come of age, it's time you had some financial responsibility . . . Happy birthday.'

Frederick handed an envelope to his son. Inside was a certificate for £8,000 worth of unit trusts. 'I don't know what to say, Dad,' gasped Colin in surprise.

'Well, thank-you might be a start. It's not a trivial gift, you know – though at least I didn't have to pay any capital gains tax on it.'

Chapter 5 looked at gifts that are exempt from inheritance tax and capital gains tax (CGT). However, even if you give away an asset which is not exempt from (CGT) – for example, a gift of shares, unit trusts, a second home, or a valuable heirloom – you may still not have to pay any tax, for the following reasons:

- Increases in the value of an asset in line with inflation are not taxed.
- You can deduct various expenses from a gain before it's assessed for tax.
- You can reduce gains on some assets by deducting losses made on various other assets.
- You are allowed to make several £'000s of gains tax-free each year.

Your first step is to work out whether or not you have made a taxable gain on the asset you are giving away – the sums vary depending on when you first started to own the asset.

CGT on gifts of assets acquired since March 1982

For an asset that you started to own on or after 31 March 1982:

- Take the 'final value' of the gift. This will usually be the price you would have received if you had sold the asset in the open market.
- *Less* the 'initial value' of the gift. This is the price you originally paid for the asset, or its market value at the time you first became the owner.
- *Less* any 'allowable expenses'. These are costs you incurred in acquiring and disposing of the asset and expenses incurred for the purpose of enhancing the value of an asset, such as commission paid to a broker, the cost of an expert valuation, and solicitors' fees, but not spending on maintenance or repairs.
- *Less* an 'indexation allowance'. The initial value and each allowable expense are multiplied by an 'indexation factor'. The results of these sums are added together and the total is your indexation allowance. It tells you how much of the increase in the value of the asset is a gain purely in line with inflation. These gains due to inflation are not usually taxed. But from 6 April 1995 indexation allowances will no longer be allowed to create or increase a loss for CGT. From 30 November 1993 until then, such losses are restricted to a maximum of £10,000.

The result of this calculation is your 'chargeable gain'. If the answer is less than zero, you have made an 'allowable loss'.

EXAMPLE 6.1

On his 18th birthday on 1 November 1993, Colin is given a holding of unit trusts by his father, Frederick. The units were originally bought by Frederick in July 1987 for £4,700. They are now worth £8,500. As Frederick is 'disposing' of the holding, there could be a CGT bill. To work out whether he has made a chargeable gain, Frederick makes the following calculations:

Final value of unit trusts	£8,500
less initial value	£4,700
less fee paid to investment adviser at the time the units were bought	£150
less indexation allowance – see below	£1,892
Chargeable gain	£1,758

The indexation allowance is calculated as follows:

Initial value in July 1987	£4,700
plus allowable expenses incurred at the time of acquisition – in this case: fee paid to an investment adviser	£150
Total initial value	£4,850
Indexation factor provided by Inland Revenue (see p. 64)	0.390
Indexation allowance ($£4,850 \times 0.390$)	£1,892

EXAMPLE 6.2

Sylvia and Jeffrey decide to give their elder daughter, Hazel, an oil painting she has asked for (see p. 49). It has been in Sylvia's family for several generations and is worth £7,000.

The gift counts as a disposal of a 'chattel' with a predicted life of more than 50 years. Its value is greater than £6,000, so there may be a CGT bill (see p. 50), but special rules apply in calculating the chargeable gain: the gain will be the *lower* of either five-thirds of the excess of the disposal value over £6,000 or the gain worked out in the normal way.

When Sylvia inherited the painting in 1987, it was valued at £3,500. Sylvia can claim an indexation allowance (see p. 64) of

£1,200. For simplicity, assume there are no allowable expenses. The two calculations are as follows:

Method 1

Final value	£7,000
less £6,000	£6,000
	£1,000
5/3 × £1,000	£1,667

Method 2

Final value	£7,000
less initial value	£3,500
less indexation allowance	£1,200
	£2,300

Method 1 gives the lowest answer, so Sylvia's chargeable gain is £1,667.

CGT on gifts of assets acquired before April 1982

Gains due to inflation were not always tax-free. The legislation taking them out of the CGT net is effective only from the end of March 1982 onwards. For an asset which you started to own *before* 1 April 1982 (or 6 April 1982 in the case of shares), the sums are slightly different from those outlined in the previous section. There are two methods of calculating your chargeable gain, as follows:

- *Method 1* The initial value is usually taken to be the value of the asset on 31 March 1982, and the indexation allowance for the initial cost is based on inflation since that date. Any allowable expenses incurred before 31 March 1982 are ignored; allowable expenses after that date are indexed in the normal way.

- *Method 2* If working out your chargeable gain using Method 1 would result in a higher CGT bill than taking into account the full period during which you have owned the asset, you can instead work out the chargeable gain based on the whole period. In this case, the initial value is the actual value at the time you first acquired the asset. The indexation allowance is worked out based on either the initial value *or* the asset's value on 31 March 1982 but adjusting for inflation only since March 1982.

If Method 1 and Method 2 both result in a gain, your chargeable gain will be the lower of the two amounts. If both methods give a loss, your allowable loss is the smaller amount. If one gives a gain and the other a loss, you are deemed to have made neither a gain nor a loss – there will be no CGT to pay but no loss to offset against gains on other assets.

You can elect to use just Method 1. If you do, *all* your assets will be covered by the election. The effect is as if you had sold all your assets on 31 March 1982 and immediately rebought them. It will usually be worth making the election if the values of all or most of your assets were higher on 31 March 1982 than they were at the time you first acquired them.

EXAMPLE 6.3

Tom's grandmother, Emily, gives Tom some shares as a wedding present in November 1993. She originally bought them in 1979 for £1,500 and they are now worth £3,500. On 31 March 1982, they were valued at just £1,000. Emily's chargeable gain is worked out using Methods 1 and 2, as follows:

Method 1

Final value of shares	£3,500
less value of shares on 31 March 1982	£1,000
less indexation allowance (see below)	£782
Chargeable gain	£1,718

Method 2

Final value of shares	£3,500
less initial value of shares	£1,500
less indexation allowance	£1,173
Chargeable gain	£827

Indexation allowances:

Indexation factor for inflation since 31 March 1982	0.782
Method 1: Indexation allowance using value at 31 March 1982 (0.782 × £1,000)	£782
Method 2: Indexation allowance using initial value (0.782 × £1,500)	£1,173

The result is smaller using Method 2, so Emily's chargeable gain is £827.

Working out your indexation allowance

The Inland Revenue publishes a monthly press release that gives details of indexation factors for current disposals of assets. You can get details from your usual tax office or a local Tax Enquiry Centre (see 'Inland Revenue' in the phone book), or through some newspapers and magazines.

If you need the indexation factor for disposals made earlier, you can work it out from the Retail Prices Index (RPI). This index is the most commonly used measure of the level of prices in Great Britain; it is published each month by the Department of Employment. You can find RPI figures in the *Department of Employment Gazette* which should be available at larger reference libraries and on teletext services. Table 6.1 lists the RPI from March 1982 up to the time this book went to press.

To work out the appropriate indexation factor, take the RPI figure for the month in which you dispose of the asset – call this R_D

Table 6.1 Retail Prices Index (Base: January 1987 = 100)

	1982	1983	1984	1985	1986	1987	1988	1989	1990	1991	1992	1993
January	–	82.61	86.84	91.20	96.25	100.0	103.3	111.0	119.5	130.2	135.6	137.9
February	–	82.97	87.20	91.94	96.60	100.4	103.7	111.8	120.2	130.9	136.3	138.8
March	79.44	83.12	87.48	92.80	96.73	100.6	104.1	112.3	121.4	131.4	136.7	139.3
April	81.04	84.28	88.64	94.78	97.67	101.8	105.8	114.3	125.1	133.1	138.8	140.6
May	81.62	84.64	88.97	95.21	97.85	101.9	106.2	115.0	126.2	133.5	139.3	141.1
June	81.85	84.84	89.20	95.41	97.79	101.9	106.6	115.4	126.7	134.1	139.3	141.0
July	81.88	85.30	89.10	95.23	97.52	101.8	106.7	115.5	126.8	133.8	138.8	140.7
August	81.90	85.68	89.94	95.49	97.82	102.1	107.9	115.8	128.1	134.1	138.9	141.3
September	81.85	86.06	90.11	95.44	98.30	102.4	108.4	116.6	129.3	134.6	139.4	141.9
October	82.26	86.36	90.67	95.59	98.45	102.9	109.5	117.5	130.3	135.1	139.9	141.8
November	82.66	86.67	90.95	95.92	99.29	103.4	110.0	118.5	130.0	135.6	139.7	141.6
December	82.51	86.89	90.87	96.05	99.62	103.3	110.3	118.8	129.9	135.7	139.2	141.6

– and the RPI figure for the month in which you acquired the asset (or incurred the expense), or for March 1982, whichever is appropriate – call this R_I. Then make the following calculation:

$$\text{Indexation factor} = \frac{R_D - R_I}{R_I}$$

Indexation factors are calculated to the nearest three decimal places. See also page 60 for new rules on indexation allowances and losses.

EXAMPLE 6.4

Emily gave Tom some shares in November 1993. She originally acquired them in July 1979, but she can claim an indexation allowance only for the period since March 1982. To work out the allowance, she takes the RPI for November 1993 which is 141.6 (see Table 6.1 on p.65) and the RPI for March 1982 which is 79.44. She does the following sum:

$$\text{Indexation factor} = \frac{R_D - R_I}{R_I} = \frac{141.6 - 79.44}{79.44}$$
$$= 0.782$$

The indexation *factor* Emily needs to use is 0.782. She can work out the indexation *allowance* by multiplying the asset value or allowable expense by the indexation factor.

Shares and unit trusts

If you give away identical shares, unit trusts, or other securities that you bought (or acquired in some other way) all at the same time, the CGT rules apply in the same way as for any other asset. However, suppose you own shares in one company, all of the same type, but they were bought at different times; there are special rules for working out which shares you are disposing of. Your share holding is divided into a maximum of five 'batches', as follows:

- *Batch 1* Your disposal is matched first to shares which you bought on the same day as the disposal. You cannot claim any indexation allowance.

- *Batch 2* Next, your disposal is matched to shares which you bought within 10 days before the disposal. You cannot claim any indexation allowance.

- *Batch 3* Next, the disposal is matched to a 'pool' made up of all shares you acquired on or after 6 April 1982. To find the initial value of the shares and your indexation allowance, you need to work out the value of the shares after indexation *for the pool as a whole* (see Example 6.5 below).

- *Batch 4* Next, the disposal is matched to a 'pool' made up of all the shares you bought in the period 6 April 1965 up to 5 April 1982. Again, to value the shares, you need to look at the pool as a whole. The indexation allowance is calculated only from March 1982, but based either on the actual purchases you made or on the value at 31 March 1982, unless you have elected to have all your assets rebased to this date (see pp. 62–63).

- *Batch 5* Finally, the disposal is matched to any shares which you acquired before 6 April 1965 starting with the shares you bought most recently and working backwards. You can opt to have quoted shares treated as part of batch 4 instead.

EXAMPLE 6.5

In November 1993, Emily also gave Tom 1,000 shares in another company, valued at £3,000. These are part of a holding which Emily originally acquired in two lots: 1,000 shares for £1,500 in June 1982 and 2,000 shares for £4,000 in March 1988. The shares form a 'batch 3 pool'. The initial value of the pool after indexation is worked out as follows:

Cost of 1,000 shares bought in June 1982	£1,500
plus indexation allowance for period June 1982 to November 1993 (0.730 × £1,500)	£1,095
plus cost of 2,000 shares bought in March 1988	£4,000
plus indexation allowance for period March 1988 to November 1993 (0.360 × £4,000)	£1,440
Indexed value of pool	£8,035

Emily is giving away 1,000 of the 3,000 shares in the pool. The indexed value of the shares she gives away is deemed to be $1000/3000 \times £8,035 = £2,678$. (The indexed value of the shares remaining in the pool is $2000/3000 \times £8,035 = £5,357$ as at November 1993 – further indexation allowance will accrue up to the time Emily disposes of these shares.) Emily's chargeable gain on the gift to Tom is worked out as follows:

Value of shares at the time of the gift	£3,000
less indexed value of the shares	£2,586
Chargeable gain	£414

How much tax?

Once you've calculated your chargeable gains and allowable losses for the tax year, you can see if there is any CGT to pay by working through the following steps:

- *Deduct* any allowable losses made in the tax year from any chargeable gains. This gives you your 'net chargeable gains'. If you have made a net loss for the year, you can carry it forward to set against gains in future years.
- If you have made net chargeable gains, *deduct* the tax-free slice. The first slice of your gains each year is tax-free: in both the 1993–94 and 1994–95 tax years, you can have net taxable gains of up to £5,800 before any CGT is payable.
- If your net chargeable gains come to more than £5,800, *deduct* any allowable losses made in earlier years. But do not reduce your gains below the £5,800 tax-free slice. If you still have unused allowable losses, you can continue to carry them forward to future years.

If, after following these steps, you are left with a gain, there will be tax to pay. CGT is currently charged at three rates: 20 per cent, 25 per cent and 40 per cent. To see which rate applies to you, add your taxable gains (after all the adjustments described above) to your taxable *income* for the year. The result of this sum tells you what rate of CGT is payable:

This tax rate applies	If your gains plus income equal:	
	1993–94 tax year	1994–95 tax year
20 per cent	£2,500 or less	£3,000 or less
25 per cent	More than £2,500 but less than £23,700	More than £3,000 but less than £23,700
40 per cent	£23,700 or more	£23,700 or more

If your taxable income is below a threshold and adding the gain to it takes the total above the threshold, you will pay the lower tax rate on part of your gain and the higher rate on the rest. For example, if you have taxable income of £2,100 in the 1993–94 tax year and taxable gains of £1,000 (making a total of £3,100), you would pay 20 per cent CGT on £400 of the gain and 25 per cent CGT on the £600 of gain which lies above the threshold.

EXAMPLE 6.6

Frederick made a chargeable gain of £1,758 on the unit trusts he gives to Colin (see p. 61). But after taking account of chargeable gains on other assets he's disposed of during the tax year, Frederick still has £2,500 of his tax-free slice unused. He can set part of this against the gift to Colin, which means there will be no CGT to pay.

EXAMPLE 6.7

In the 1994–95 tax year, Emily makes total chargeable gains of £12,300 and allowable losses of £2,800. Subtracting the losses from the gains leaves net chargeable gains of £9,500. Emily deducts the tax-free slice of £5,800, leaving taxable gains of £3,700. She has losses of £1,500 carried forward from earlier years; subtracting these reduces her taxable gains to £2,200.

Emily's taxable income for the year is £22,400. Adding her gains to this takes her over the £23,700 threshold, so tax on her gains is worked out as follows:

Slice of gains in excess of the £23,700 threshold	£900
CGT at 25 per cent on £1,300	£325
CGT at 40 per cent on £900	£360
Total CGT bill	£685

Hold-over relief

If you make a gift to an individual or to a trust that counts as a chargeable gift[27] for inheritance tax (IHT) purposes (see Chapter 7) and is not a potentially exempt transfer (PET) (see p. 57) under the IHT rules, then you and the recipient can jointly apply to the Inland Revenue for 'hold-over relief'. This means that, instead of realising a gain on the asset you give, and paying tax on that gain, you – in effect – give away your CGT liability along with the asset.

It works likes this. At the time of the gift, the chargeable gain you have made on the asset is worked out; relief is given by deducting the gain from your total of chargeable gains for the year, thus you pay no CGT on it. The chargeable gain is also deducted from the recipient's initial value of the gift. This reduces the initial value and so increases the likelihood of a chargeable gain when the recipient comes to dispose of the asset.

Before 14 March 1989, hold-over relief applied to a much wider range of gifts, including those which counted as PETs under the IHT legislation. The restrictions now applying to the relief mean that it is mainly useful when you are making gifts to a discretionary trust (see p. 98).

Giving away the family business

Hold-over relief is also available when you give away assets used in your business or shares in a family company. Once again, relief must be claimed jointly by both the giver and the recipient. It works by enabling the giver to deduct the gain which would otherwise be payable from their chargeable gains, and the recipient deducts the

---

[27] Or would do so, but for the use of one or more of the IHT exemptions (see pp. 53–56).

Giving away the family business

Hold-over relief is also available when you give away assets used in your business or shares in a family company. Once again, relief must be claimed jointly by both the giver and the recipient. It works by enabling the giver to deduct the gain which would otherwise be payable from their chargeable gains, and the recipient deducts the same amount from the initial value at which they receive the assets or shares.

If the assets concerned have not been used in the business for the whole time that they were owned by the giver, then the amount of hold-over relief available may be scaled down proportionately (and the relevant period of ownership includes any time before 31 March 1982).

If hold-over relief is available on the assets anyway because they are subject to an IHT charge (see above) then the IHT-related hold-over relief applies rather than the business-related relief. Similarly, if the assets or shares qualify for 'retirement relief' (which reduces or eliminates a CGT bill that would otherwise be payable when you dispose of your business in order to retire[28]), this will be given in preference to hold-over relief.

Hold-over relief can also be claimed on gifts of agricultural property. If the land or property is not currently in use as part of your business, then relief may still be granted if the property also qualifies for relief from IHT (see p. 83).

If you are planning to give away your business or farm, you should seek advice from your accountant and solicitor.

Telling the taxman

There is a section on your tax return which asks about capital gains and losses made during the tax year. If you do not receive a tax return, you should write to your tax office with details of your capital gains, if:

---

[28]Retirement relief is outside the scope of this book. For further details see, for example, *Which? Way to Save Tax 1994*, Consumers' Association, 1994.

- your gains come to more than the tax-free slice (£5,800 for 1994–95), *or*
- the final value of assets you have disposed of during the year exceeds twice the amount of the tax-free slice (i.e. £11,600 for 1994–95).

If you are not asked for details earlier, you must notify the tax office within 12 months of the end of the tax year concerned. Tax on gains will normally be due on 1 December following the year of assessment (i.e. usually the year in which you make the gains).

CHAPTER 7

INHERITANCE TAX ON LIFETIME GIFTS

A TAX NO ONE PAYS?

'Do you have to pay any inheritance tax when you give me Hadley Hall?' asked Albert.

'It's none of your business,' snapped Daisy, 'though if you'd bothered to learn anything useful you'd know that there's no inheritance tax on a gift from one person to another – it's a PET! I suppose you think that's a furry animal.'

'As it happens I *do* know about PETs,' retorted Albert, 'and there could be a tax bill – what's more I could end up having to pay it. So it really is my business too.'

Chapter 5 listed the many exemptions from inheritance tax (IHT) for gifts made during your lifetime – so many in fact that IHT is sometimes referred to as a voluntary tax. That is not quite true. There are two main types of gift that could result in an IHT bill during the giver's lifetime, as follows:

1. Gifts to or from a company.
2. Gifts to a 'discretionary trust' (see p. 98).

Gifts from one person to another, which counted as potentially exempt transfers (PETS) (see p. 57) when they were made, can also cause an IHT bill if the person making the gift dies within seven years. You must also be careful if you make 'gifts with reservation': that is, giving away something from which you continue to benefit.

Gifts which are taxable when they are made

The scope of inheritance tax

The forerunner of IHT was called capital transfer tax (CTT). The two taxes were virtually the same, with one very important difference: CTT applied to virtually *all* gifts, whereas under the IHT system, gifts between *individuals* (and certain types of trust) count as PETs, which are tax-free as long as the giver survives for seven years after making the gift. However, even under the present system, some gifts – that is, those which are *not* between individuals (and certain trusts) – can prompt an immediate tax bill. In tax language, such gifts are called 'chargeable transfers' and they comprise mainly gifts involving companies and gifts to discretionary trusts. In this book, chargeable transfers are also referred to as 'chargeable gifts'.

How a chargeable transfer is taxed

IHT does not apply to each gift you make in isolation. It is based on all the chargeable transfers you have made over the last seven years. Adding all these gifts together gives you a 'cumulative total' – called your 'running total' in this book. The first slice of the running total – up to £150,000 for the 1994–95 tax year – is tax-free. You pay tax only on gifts which take you above that limit. The tax-free slice is normally increased each tax year in line with inflation up to the previous December, but, for 1992–93, the tax-free slice was increased by more than inflation and in the two subsequent years it was not increased at all.

The IHT rate on lifetime gifts is set with reference to the rate of tax which may apply to your estate when you die (see Chapter 11). The death rate for the 1994–95 tax year is 40 per cent; the lifetime rate is half that (i.e. 20 per cent).

Tax due on a lifetime gift can be paid either by the person (or trust or company) making the gift or by the person (or trust or company) receiving the gift. If the person making the gift pays the tax, the tax itself counts as part of the gift, which increases the value of the transfer to be taxed. A gift where the giver pays the tax is called a 'net gift'; if the recipient pays the tax, it is called a 'gross gift'. You can work out how much tax is due on a net or gross gift using the calculators opposite.

INHERITANCE TAX CALCULATOR FOR NET GIFTS

A   What is your running total before making the gift (including any tax paid by you)?

B   Work out the tax due on your running total:
If **A** is £150,000 or less, the tax due is 0.
If **A** is more than £150,000, the tax due is 20% × [**A** – £150,000].

C   Subtract **B** from **A**. This gives you your *net* running total.

D   Enter value of gift – use the amount the recipient will receive.

E   Add **C** and **D**. This gives you your new net running total.

F   Work out the tax due on your new running total:
If **E** is £150,000 or less, the tax is 0.
If **E** is more than £150,000, the tax due is ¼ × [**E** – £150,000].

G   Subtract **B** from **F**. This is the amount of tax (to be paid by the giver) on the current gift.

INHERITANCE TAX ON A GROSS GIFT

A   What is your running total before making the gift (including any tax paid by you)?

B   Work out the tax due on your running total:
If **A** is £150,000 or less, the tax due is 0.
If **A** is more than £150,000, the tax due is 20% × [**A** – £150,000].

C   Enter the current gift – use the amount you are giving.

D   Find your new running total by adding **C** and **A**.

E   Work out the tax due on your new running total:
If **D** is £150,000 or less, the tax due is 0.
If **D** is more than £150,000, the tax due is 20% × [**D** – £150,000].

F   Subtract **B** from **E**. This is the amount of tax (to be paid by the recipient) on the current gift.

EXAMPLE 7.1

Frederick has a grown-up daughter, Louise, who suffers from a slight mental disability. She lives largely independently and has a modest income from a job in a supermarket, but she would not be able to cope with large sums of money or complicated planning for the future.

Frederick wants to make sure that Louise will always be financially secure and to provide a 'last resort' emergency fund which would be available to his son Colin if the need arose. Frederick decides to set up a discretionary trust for the benefit of his children, making himself and his sister the trustees who will decide when Louise or Colin need help and how much help they should receive. (For more about discretionary trusts, see Chapter 9.)

Frederick sets up the trust in May 1994 with a gift of £60,000. He will pay any tax due on this, so it is a net gift. As Frederick has not used any of his annual exemption of £3,000 for 1994–95 (see p. 55), only £57,000 counts as a chargeable transfer. Over the seven years from June 1987 to May 1994, he has made other chargeable transfers of £98,000. He uses the calculator for net gifts (see previous page) to work out his inheritance tax position as follows:

A Frederick's running total before making the gift (including any tax paid by him).	£98,000
B Tax due on his running total: If **A** is £150,000 or less, the tax due is 0. If **A** is more than £150,000, the tax due is 20% × [**A** – £150,000]	£0
C Subtract **B** from **A**. This gives you Frederick's *net* running total	£98,000
D Enter value of gift – the amount the trust will receive	£57,000
E Add **C** and **D**. This gives Frederick's new net running total	£155,000
F Tax due on his new running total: If **E** is £150,000 or less, the tax is 0 If **E** is more than £150,000, the tax is due is ¼ × [**E** – £150,000] (i.e. ¼ × £5,000)	£1,250
G Subtract **B** from **F**. This is the amount of tax (to be paid by Frederick) on the gift to the trust.	£1,250

Frederick's gift to the trust is made up of the £60,000 plus £1,250 he pays in tax – £61,250 in total.

Example 7.2

Suppose, in Example 7.1 above, that Frederick decided to pay £60,000 into the trust, but to leave the trust to pay any tax. In this case, the chargeable transfer of £57,000 would be a *gross* gift. Using the calculator for gross gifts (see p. 75), the inheritance tax position would be:

A Frederick's running total before making the gift (including any tax paid by him)	£98,000
B Tax due on his running total: If **A** is £150,000 or less, the tax due is 0. If **A** is more than £150,000, the tax due is 20% × [**A** – £150,000]	£0
C Enter the current gift – the amount Frederick is giving	£57,000
D Frederick's new running total is found by adding **C** and **A**	£155,000
E Tax due on his new running total: If **D** is £150,000 or less, the tax due is 0. If **D** is more than £150,000, the tax due is 20% × [**D** – £150,000].)	£1,000 (i.e. 20% × £5000)
F Subtract **B** from **E**. This is the amount of tax (to be paid by the trust) on the gift to the trust.	£1,000

The trust would receive £60,000, but £1,000 would have to be used to pay the IHT Bill due on the transfer.

Death within seven years

Tax on a lifetime gift which is a chargeable transfer is usually charged at a rate of 20 per cent (in 1994–95). But, if the person making the gift dies within three years, the gift is reassessed and tax is charged at the full death rate current at the time of death (i.e. 40 per cent for 1994–95). If the giver dies more than three years but less than seven years after making the gift, the gift is still reassessed for tax but at less than the full death rate. Table 7.1 shows the rates which would apply.

The extra tax due will be charged to the person who received the gift, but if they cannot or will not pay, the giver's estate must pay the bill.

Table 7.1   New tax rate if giver dies within seven years of making a gift

Years between gift and death	% of full death rate which applies	% rate of tax on the gift (at 1992–93 rates)
Up to 3	100	40
More than 3 and up to 4	80	32
More than 4 and up to 5	60	24
More than 5 and up to 6	40	16
More than 6 up to 7	20	8
More than 7	0	no extra tax

At first sight, you might assume that there will never be any extra tax to pay if the giver dies more than five years after making the chargeable transfer, since the rate of tax which would then apply (16 per cent assuming 1994–95 rates) is lower than the 20 per cent rate at which tax is paid on lifetime gifts. However, the position is not so simple: in reassessing the gift, it is looked at in relation to the running total at the time the gift was made; since PETs may also be reassessed (see opposite) when the giver dies, a PET made within the seven-year period but before the chargeable transfer being considered would increase the running total. Also, bear in mind that the original tax on the gift was charged at the rates applicable at the time of the gift, whereas tax due on reassessment is charged at the rates applicable at the time of death – and a change in rates may result in extra tax becoming due. For a summary of tax-free slices and tax rates applicable in earlier years, see Appendix, p. 155.

Potentially exempt transfers (PETs)

As discussed above, most of the gifts you make in your lifetime are likely to be PETs. There is no IHT to pay at the time a PET is given, and no IHT at all if the giver then survives for seven years. If, however, the giver dies within seven years of making the gift, it is reassessed and an IHT bill *may* follow.

Whether or not there is IHT to pay depends on the pattern of chargeable transfers made by the late giver during the seven years before the PET was originally made. For example:

- There will be no IHT if the giver had unused yearly tax-free exemption for the year in which the PET was made (plus any unused yearly exemption carried forward from the year before that) and the exemption is at least as much as the value of the gift.
- There will be no IHT if the giver's running total including the PET for the seven years up to the date when the PET was made is less than the tax-free slice which applies at the time of death.

If any unused yearly exemption and/or tax-free slice is smaller than the amount of the gift, then there will be IHT to pay on the reassessment of the PET.

Note that PETs within seven years of death may become taxable and that transfers during the seven years up to the time the PET was made affect the assessment. Thus gifts made up to *fourteen* years before death can affect the amount of tax that becomes due at the time of death.

How is a PET taxed?

When someone dies, all the PETs they made in the last seven years before death are looked at again and reclassed as chargeable transfers. This has two effects: first, there may be tax to pay on the PET itself; secondly, the PET is added to the cumulative total of transfers and may affect tax due on other PETs, extra tax due on chargeable transfers that were made after the PET in question and tax on the estate (see Chapter 11).

If the giver dies within three years of making a PET, IHT is charged at the full death rate. But if the death occurs between three and seven years after death, IHT is levied at only a proportion of the death rate. Table 7.2 shows the tax rates which would apply.

As with chargeable transfers, the extra tax due on a PET which becomes chargeable is first charged to the person who received the gift. If they cannot or will not pay, the late giver's estate must pay the bill.

Table 7.2 New tax rate if giver dies within seven years of making a gift

Years between gift and death	% of full death rate which applies	% rate of tax on the gift (at 1992–93 rates)
Up to 3	100	40
More than 3 and up to 4	80	32
More than 4 and up to 5	60	24
More than 5 and up to 6	40	16
More than 6 and up to 7	20	8
More than 7	0	no tax

EXAMPLE 7.3

Lydia made a gift of £74,000 to a discretionary trust in December 1988. At the time, there was no tax to pay because Lydia was able to set her yearly tax-free exemption of £3,000 against part of the gift and the tax-free slice, which was £71,000 in 1986–87, against the rest.

Lydia dies in July 1994. The gift to the discretionary trust is reviewed – and so is a PET of £139,000 which Lydia made in August 1988. The gifts are reassessed as follows:

Running total just before PET in August 1988	£0
plus PET now a chargeable gift	£139,000
	£139,000

(Note: no tax on the former PET, as it is less than unused tax-free slice)

plus gift to discretionary trust in December 1988	£74,000
less yearly exemption	£3,000
Running total including gift to discretionary trust	£210,000
less 1994–95 tax-free slice	£150,000
	£60,000
Tax at 1994–95 death rate of 40% (0.4 × £60,000)	£24,000
Scaled down to 40% of death rate since death occurred between five and six years after the gift (0.4 × £24,000)	£9,600
less tax already paid at time of gift	£0
Tax due on reassessment	£9,600

Protection from IHT on a PET

Life insurance can be used to protect the person receiving a PET from a possible IHT bill (see p. 149 for how this would work). The insurance could be taken out by the person making a PET, in which case the insurance would itself count as a gift but might qualify for one of the IHT exemptions (see p. 53–56). Another option would be for the person receiving the PET to pay premiums himself for a term insurance policy based on the life of the giver.

Life insurance can also be used in just the same way to protect the recipient of a gift that counts as a chargeable transfer from the possibility of an extra tax bill should the giver die within seven years.

For more information, seek advice from an insurance broker or an independent financial adviser.

Gifts with reservation

Problems can arise if you give something away but continue to benefit from it in some way. A 'gift with reservation' occurs in the following circumstances:

● If the person you give the thing to does not really take possession of it: for example, you might give a valuable painting to someone but insist that it carries on hanging in your home.

● If you carry on deriving some benefit from the thing you give away unless you pay a full market rate – or the equivalent in kind – for your use of the asset. This might occur, for example, if you give your home to your children but you retain the right to live in part of the property rent-free.

There are special rules which apply to gifts with reservation. However, if the gift is covered by one of the exemptions outlined on pages 53 to 56 at the time the gift is made, the special rules do not normally apply and there is no IHT to pay. But you cannot claim the 'expenditure out of normal income' exemption against a gift with reservation and you cannot use your £3,000 yearly exemption against the gift at the time it is made.

Unless the gift counts as a chargeable transfer, there is no IHT to pay when the gift is made, but there may be later on. The special rules come into operation at the time the person who made the gift dies. If, at the time of death, the giver still benefited from the gift with reservation, the possessions they gave are treated as if they are still part of the giver's estate and were given away only at the time of death (see Chapter 11). If the giver stopped benefiting from the possessions some time before his death, the gift with reservation is treated as a PET made at the time the giver's benefit stopped. Provided that this was more than seven years before death, IHT will not apply. On the other hand, if that time was within the seven years before the giver's death, the normal PET rules apply and there may be an IHT bill on the gift. In the event that the giver had unused yearly exemption for the year in which the gift stopped being a gift with reservation, that can be set against the PET in the normal way.

If the gift with reservation counted as a chargeable transfer, IHT may have been paid when the gift was made – this would apply, say, to a gift you made to a discretionary trust. The special rules still apply when the giver dies, but other rules prevent IHT being payable twice over on the same gift. For example, suppose you give £10,000 to a discretionary trust designed to benefit your whole family, including yourself. Because you are a beneficiary of the trust, you are still able to benefit from the £10,000 so it counts as a gift with reservation. As a gift to a discretionary trust, it is a chargeable transfer on which IHT may be payable. But, if you continue to be a beneficiary of the trust right up to the time you die, the £10,000 will continue to be deemed as part of your estate and treated as if it was given outright to the trust only on the date of your death. At that time, the gift may again give rise to an IHT bill, but special rules give you relief against the double charge (though not against other tax charges relating to the trust, see pp. 103–106).

A gift is not a gift with reservation if you continue to benefit but you pay for the right to do so. For example, you might give away your house but buy a lease at a full market rate which lets you live in the house for some specified period – maybe long enough to cover the rest of your expected life – or you might offer services, for example, as housekeeper and gardener, that are equivalent in value to the market rent for the property you continue to occupy.

A gift of a house or other real property is also not a gift with reservation if the giver's enjoyment of the property arises out of an unforeseen change in circumstances, and the giver is a relation of either the recipient or their husband or wife. For example, you might give the family home to your children while you move to somewhere smaller; but, some years later, your health fails and you have to move in with your children so that they can look after you. As long as this represents reasonable care and maintenance of you by your children, the 'reservation' element of the gift will be ignored.

Your husband or wife can benefit from a gift you make to someone else without the reservation rules applying as long as you can show that you do not benefit from your spouse's enjoyment of the gift.

If you can carve up a possession which you intend to give so that you can keep a distinct part of it, you can give away the remainder without that part counting as a gift with reservation.

Giving away the family business

If you pass on your business or farm during your lifetime, you may qualify for relief against IHT on the value of the transfer. Basic details of the schemes are given on pp. 137–139, which look at passing on your business or farm in your will. The application of the scheme is broadly the same in the case of lifetime gifts, with one important exception that is outlined below.

Whether your gift of business or agricultural property counts as a PET or as a chargeable transfer, the relief will be clawed back, if:

- you die within seven years of making the gift, and
- the recipient no longer owns the business or farm, and
- the recipient does not fully re-invest the proceeds in – in the case of business property relief – a new business, or – in the case of agricultural property relief – a new farm.

Relief will also be clawed back if the recipient dies before you and no longer owns the business or farm.

In view of this clawback, it is extremely important that you plan carefully, and that you take expert advice from your accountant and a solicitor, before making a gift of part or all of your business or farm.

Telling the taxman

For 1994–95 you do not need to tell the tax authorities about gifts you make provided:

- your total chargeable transfers during the year come to no more than £10,000, and
- your running total of gifts during the last seven years comes to no more than £40,000.

You do not have to tell them about PETs you make. If you die within seven years of making a PET, the recipient is required to report the gift within 12 months of your death. Nor do you have to report chargeable gifts you make that are *entirely* covered by one or more of the tax-free exemptions listed in Chapter 5 or fall *entirely* within the tax-free slice of your running total.

If you made a gift with reservation, the recipient must report the gift within 12 months of your death, if the reservation persisted up to the time of your death.

If you have made a chargeable transfer that should be reported, you need to complete **Form IHT100**, which is available from the Capital Taxes Office (see Useful addresses).

In the case of lifetime chargeable gifts, IHT is normally due to be paid six months after the end of the month in which the gift was made. But if the gift was made in the period 6 April to 1 October, tax is due on 30 April of the following year.

Should extra tax become payable on a chargeable gift, or should PET become chargeable, because of the death of the giver within seven years of making the gift, the tax is due six months after the end of the month in which the death occurs. In some limited cases, it may be possible to pay the tax in ten equal yearly instalments.

CHAPTER 8

INCOME TAX AND GIFTS

WHOSE TAX IS IT ANYWAY?

'I don't believe this,' exploded Michael, waving the tax assessment he had just opened. 'The Revenue have charged me income tax on Rebecca's savings account.'

Rebecca looked on quizzically. 'But you opened the account for me, Daddy. Isn't it mine any more?'

There is no income tax as such on a gift, but just as a gift to charity can affect the income tax position of the giver and the recipient, so too can gifts between individuals. If you are aware of the types of gift that affect income tax and the pitfalls to watch out for, you are then well placed to arrange your giving in the most tax-efficient way.

Gifts between husband and wife

Independent taxation

An important date in the tax calendar was 6 April 1990, because, from the 1990–91 tax year onwards, 'independent taxation' was introduced. A married couple had up to then been treated as a single unit for tax purposes, but now husband and wife are each treated as individuals responsible for their own tax. This means that:

● You are taxed on your own income, regardless of your spouse's income.

- You claim your own tax allowances to set against your income.
- You have your own tax-free slice for capital gains tax (CGT) purposes. (You also have your own inheritance tax (IHT) running total and exemptions, but this was the case even before independent taxation was introduced.)

Before independent taxation, it mattered little from an income tax point of view whether it was you or your husband or wife who owned the family assets – house, savings, and so on. Any income from such assets was always treated as that of the husband even if legally it belonged to the wife. Under the new system, your individual tax bills will take account of income from the assets that each of you in fact own. Who owns what is important now and rearranging the family assets – for example, through gifts between husband and wife – could reduce the income tax bill of the family as a whole. Bear in mind that there is no CGT or IHT to pay on gifts between husband and wife, but the pattern in which you hold the family assets could affect IHT later on (see Chapter 12).

EXAMPLE 8.1

Until early in 1990, all the family investments had been in Ray's name and his wife, Joyce, had had no income or savings of her own. Ray pays tax at the basic rate of 25 per cent, so with the advent of independent taxation, it made sense for Ray to give Joyce some of the income-producing investments. This means that she now has enough income to set against her personal tax allowance (which is £3,445 in 1994–95). There was no IHT or CGT to pay on the gift from Ray to Joyce.

Jointly owned assets

Like many married couples, you may well have bank accounts, savings accounts and investments that are jointly held by you and your husband or wife. There are two ways of holding assets jointly: under a 'joint tenancy' or as 'tenants in common'. (These are legal terms which can apply to any type of asset and not just the way you share a home.)

Under a joint tenancy, you and your spouse both own the whole asset, you have identical interests in it, and you cannot sell or give away the asset without the agreement of the other person. In the event of one of you dying, the other automatically becomes the sole owner of the asset (though the deceased person's share still counts as part of his or her estate).

Under a tenancy in common, you and your spouse both have the right to enjoy or use the whole asset, but you each have your own distinct share in the asset and the shares need not be equal. On your death, your share of the asset does not automatically pass to your husband or wife and you can leave it to anyone you choose.

You can switch from owning an asset under a joint tenancy to a tenancy in common quite simply. The switch does not need to be recorded in any particular legal form – a simple written statement from one owner to the other would be sufficient. However, it is better for a joint statement to be agreed and signed by both owners. Switching from a tenancy in common to a joint tenancy requires a formal deed, which a solicitor can draw up for you.

For income tax purposes, the Inland Revenue will at first assume that any assets you hold jointly are held under a joint tenancy. This means that you will each be treated as receiving half of any income from the asset. If you want the income to be treated differently, you need to send your tax office a completed **Form 17** setting out how the income is to be shared between you. You can get Form 17 from your usual tax office or a local Tax Enquiry Centre.

However, be warned that the way the income is split for tax purposes *must* reflect the actual shares that you and your spouse have in the income-producing asset. You cannot just choose the most convenient income split if it does not match the real shares, and you cannot choose one split for income purposes and another for capital.

You should be prepared to provide the Inland Revenue with proof of the shares you each have in an asset and thus your share of the income. The proof might be copies of application forms or documents you signed when you first had the asset, or copies of deeds or letters stating the relative shares.

Consider giving some of your assets to your husband or wife, or giving away part of your share of an asset, if to do so would mean that together you pay less tax, as in the following circumstances:

- If one of you pays income tax and the other does not – give income-producing assets to the non-taxpayer (as in Example 8.1 above.)
- If one of you pays tax at the higher rate and the other pays tax at the basic rate – give income-producing assets to the basic-rate taxpayer. (And, similarly, if one of you pays tax at the 20 per cent rate and the other pays tax at either the basic or higher rate, give income-producing assets to the 20 per cent rate taxpayer.)
- If one of you regularly uses up your capital gains tax-free slice but the other does not – give assets whose value is expected to rise to the person with the unused slice.

Gifts to children

A child is an individual for tax purposes and has his or her own personal tax allowance to set against any income. Many children do not make use of their allowance, so there is scope for reducing the family's overall tax bill by making gifts to a child. However, the tax rules are very strict in this area and any gift to a child needs to be carefully thought out if it is to have the desired income tax effect.

Gifts from parents

In general, if you give assets to your child and these produce income, the income will count as *yours* – not the child's. For example, if you invest some money in a building society for your son or daughter, interest earned will generally count as your interest. But the Inland Revenue makes a concession in the case of small amounts of income: up to £100 a year of income from assets given by a parent can count as income of the child. This concession applies to each parent, so the child could have up to £200 income from such gifts if both father and mother gave the maximum allowed.

Should you want to give more to your child without having to pay their tax bill, you have two main choices, as follows:

1. Give assets whose income is tax-free.
2. Give assets which produce capital gains rather than income.

Tax-free income

If income from gifts you have made to your child comes to more than £100 a year (£200 if you have spread the gifts equally between father and mother), and you want to make further gifts of investments, consider those which provide tax-free income: for example, certain National Savings investments, friendly society investments, or Personal Equity Plans (PEPs).

There are two investments which are especially designed for children: National Savings Children's Bonus Bonds and friendly society children's savings plans.

Children's Bonus Bonds

Children's Bonus Bonds can be bought by anyone over the age of 16 for anyone under 16. If children want to invest their own money in the bonds, they must enlist the help of their parents or some other adult. The bonds can be held until the child reaches age 21.

The minimum investment is £25, and each child can hold up to £1,000 of previous issues of bonds, plus up to £1,000 of the current issue at the time this book went to press. The money invested earns a small amount of interest, but the bulk of the return comes from bonuses which are added every five years. The interest for the next five years and the next bonus to be paid are fixed in advance and are guaranteed. On each five-year anniversary of a bond, the new interest and bonus rates are set.

The bonds automatically mature when the holder reaches 21. They can also be cashed in earlier without penalty on any five-year anniversary. If a bond is cashed in at any other time, the holder must give one month's notice and will forgo the next bonus payment.

The return on the bonds is completely tax-free. In January 1993, Children's Bonus Bonds were offering a return of 7.35 per cent a year if you held the bond for five years.

Friendly society children's savings plans

Friendly society plans are basically 10-year life insurance policies. They offer little life cover and are intended mainly as savings vehicles. Following a change in the tax rules in the 1991 Budget, from July 1991 friendly societies can offer children's savings plans aimed at people under the age of 18 – these plans are often referred to as 'baby bonds'. Either the child can invest in the plan itself, or an adult can make investments on the child's behalf.

You pay regular premiums into the plan and the society invests these in a range of assets – shares, British Government stocks, and so on. After 10 years, you receive a lump sum, the size of which reflects the growth of the underlying investments (less various charges deducted by the society). Friendly society plans are a very efficient form of investment because the society pays no tax on income and gains from the underlying investment, and *you* also pay no tax on the lump sum you receive when the plan matures. In other words the return is completely tax-free.

The drawback is that you can invest only fairly small amounts in friendly society tax-free plans. The maximum investment is £200 a year (or £18.50 a month), and you can have only one such plan at a time.

Gains rather than income

Since the restrictions applying to gifts from a parent apply only to income, you can get round them by giving assets which are expected to produce a capital gain instead. Even a child is entitled to a yearly tax-free slice for capital gains tax purposes and, as Chapter 6 described, there are various other deductions which reduce or eliminate the tax liability.

Suitable gifts might be shares that pay low or no dividends, growth unit trusts, growth investment trusts, collectors' items such as paintings and antiques, and so on.

EXAMPLE 8.2

Michael had not realised, when he opened a building society account for his daughter, Rebecca, that income from the £5,000 he had placed in the account would count as his own for tax purposes.

He decides to close the account and put £1,000 into a National Savings children's bonus bond for Rebecca, and to put the rest into a growth unit trust for her.

Gifts from friends and relatives

Income from a gift given by anyone other than a parent will count as the child's own income, so the child can set any unused personal allowance against it. You will need to be able to distinguish such gifts from those given by a parent. It would be sensible to invest the two types of gift separately: for example, small parental gifts in one building society account, gifts from other relatives and friends in another. And it is a good idea to ask people who give money or investments to your child to accompany them with a brief note stating the amount of the gift and who it is from. Keep such notes and letters in a safe place in case the Inland Revenue need to see them.

Covenants

Until March 1988, you could give money to a person under a deed of covenant and receive tax relief on the amount you gave as long as you were a taxpayer. Such arrangements were especially popular as a way of paying the parental grant contribution to a student son or daughter.

If you are still making payments under a deed of covenant which was drawn up before 15 March 1988, you continue to qualify for tax relief on the payments. These covenants work in much the same way as covenants to charities (see Chapter 3). You make a 'net' payment to the recipient: that is, you will hand over an amount that has already had tax at the basic rate deducted. If the recipient is a non-taxpayer, they claim back the tax deducted from the Inland Revenue. As long as you are a taxpayer, you keep the basic rate tax deducted from the payment – this is your tax relief. Higher-rate taxpayers cannot claim any extra relief because there is no higher-rate tax relief on covenant payments to individuals (unlike charities). If you are a non-taxpayer, the Inland Revenue will send you a bill for the tax deducted.

In the case of payments under a deed of covenant drawn up on or after the 15 March 1988, the special tax rules no longer apply. You make the payments out of your taxed income and you receive no tax relief. The recipient is not liable to tax on the amount you give, but equally cannot claim anything from the Inland Revenue even if they are a non-taxpayer.

If you have a pre-15 March 1988 covenant, avoid making changes to the deed – for example, changing the size or frequency of the payments – as these could mean the covenant then becomes covered by the new rules and would lose you the favourable tax treatment.

Since the abolition of tax relief on covenanted payments to individuals, there is no single simple method of making tax efficient gifts to an individual. If you run a business, you might consider holiday employment of a student son or daughter, say, as a way of ensuring they have enough income rather than just giving them money – their wages would be tax deductible in computing your business's profits. (But note that their earnings must be reasonable in respect to the amount and type of work they do.)

There are also a number of complex schemes (for example, sub-letting rental property to the person you would like to receive your gift so that they receive the bulk of the rental income) that are suitable only for the wealthy or those in specific circumstances. If you think such schemes might be useful for you, seek advice from a solicitor.

CHAPTER 9

USING TRUSTS

PLANNING FOR THE FUTURE

Ruth and David have become grandparents for the first time. 'I want to give the baby a nest egg for her future,' explains David to his solicitor. 'Of course, she's too young to handle money now, but I can put it in trust, can't I?'

'Yes, indeed,' replied the lawyer. 'You probably require what is known as an accumulation and maintenance trust. That would enable her to receive the money when she is adult, but gives the option to use it for her benefit in the meantime. Let us have a look at your precise circumstances and wishes.'

Trusts (which you may also come across as a form of 'settlement') are legal arrangements that enable you to give away assets but restrict or direct how and when they are used. Trusts can be used to make gifts in your lifetime and they can also be set up under the terms of a will. A trust involves three types of participant, as follows:

1. *The settlor*   This is the person who gives away the assets that are placed in the trust. A settlor can also be an organisation, and there might be more than one settlor of a trust.
2. *The beneficiary*   This is the person who is to receive the assets or benefit from them. There will be rules about when and how the benefit is to be received. A beneficiary can also be an organisation

– for example, a charity (see p. 38) – and there can be, and often is, more than one beneficiary of a trust.

3. *The trustee*   This is the person – or, more usually, people – who looks after the assets, ensuring that they are invested and used in accordance with the rules of the trust and general trust law. Both settlors and beneficiaries may act as trustees, though often independent trustees will be chosen. A corporate trustee can be appointed, but for a family trust this would usually be disproportionately expensive.

So instead of making a gift outright, using a trust enables you (the settlor) to hand assets to a third party (the trustees) who will look after the assets and pass on the gift to the recipient (the beneficiary) in accordance with whatever rules or restrictions you – or the law – have stipulated. A trust can be a useful device in a wide range of circumstances. For example:

- *Giving to children*   You want to make a gift to a child to be available to them when they are older.
- *Maintaining control*   Similarly, you might wish to give assets to someone who is not good at handling money: for example, someone with a careless financial record, or a person who is mentally infirm.
- *Giving to a group*   You wish to give to a group of people that may not yet be complete: for example, you might want all your grandchildren, some of whom may not yet be born, to share a gift.
- *Separating income from capital*   Useful where you wish to give assets to someone at some future time, but want someone else to have the use of, or income from, the assets in the meantime.
- *Giving on special occasions*   You may want to make a gift only on the occasion of some possible, but indeterminate, event, such as a marriage or birth.
- *Maintaining confidentiality*   You may want to arrange now to make a gift at some time in the future, but would prefer the beneficiary to be unaware of the gift at present.

Choosing the appropriate trust

There are three main types of trust: interest in possession trusts, discretionary trusts, and accumulation and maintenance trusts (which are in fact a special type of discretionary trust that benefit from favourable tax treatment as long as special rules are kept). Which type of trust will best suit your needs is dictated in part by the characteristics of each type of trust. Of great importance, however, is your tax position and the tax treatment of the different trusts.

The tax treatment of trusts is undoubtedly complex and there are numerous pitfalls for the unwary. The wording of the trust deed and the powers of the trustees can be crucial in assessing which tax regime applies. You are strongly advised to take advice from a solicitor before deciding on whether or not to use a trust and which type would be appropriate, and you should ask a solicitor to draw up the trust deed.[29]

The main types of trust

Interest in possession trusts

These are also known as 'fixed interest trusts' or 'life interest trusts'. They are distinct from any other type of trust because they give one or more beneficiaries the *right* to income from the assets in the trust as it arises – or the use of the assets in the case of, say, a house. Whoever eventually becomes the outright owner of the assets is said to hold a 'reversionary interest'. The same beneficiary (or beneficiaries) who receive the income may also have a reversionary interest, but this is not necessarily the case. The assets may at some future date, or on some future event, be given to some other beneficiary, or even revert to the settlor. This type of trust is commonly used in a will (see Example 9.1).

In the past, there has been debate in legal circles about precisely what counts as an 'interest in possession'. In a definitive legal case,[30] the House of Lords established guidelines, which *inter alia* state that a beneficiary does not have an interest in possession if the trustees have the power to stop the income being paid out, regardless of whether or not the trustees exercise that power. Such a trust would be classified as a discretionary trust.

---

[29]In the 'Do-It-Yourself will kits' mentioned on p. 119, some of the pro forma wills provided include clauses setting up trusts. Use these, if you are certain that the pro forma will selected reflects your wishes. If in doubt, consult a solicitor. Never try to adapt the wording of one of these wills if it does not quite match your circumstances.
[30]*Pearson* v *IRC* [1980] STC 318, [1981] AC 753.

EXAMPLE 9.1

David's will stipulates that, on his death, a large part of his assets should be placed in trust. The trustees would invest the assets as they saw fit and the income from them (and use of his former share of the family home) should go to his wife during her lifetime. On his wife's death, the assets are to be shared equally between their three children. David has drawn up his will in this way, first, to guard against his widow being short of money during her lifetime and, secondly, to ensure that his children will eventually receive his assets even if his widow remarries.

Discretionary trusts

If a trust is not an interest in possession trust, then it is by definition a discretionary trust. In general, income from the trust assets is accumulated to be paid out later to beneficiaries and/or to be paid out at the discretion of the trustees.

With discretionary trusts, there is usually more than one beneficiary and often a 'class' of beneficiaries such as your children or grandchildren.

EXAMPLE 9.2

John had been ill for some time and, knowing that he did not have long to live, he checked his will and brought it up to date. He was a widower and had six sons whose ages ranged from 22 to 30. Two of the sons had good, secure incomes, while three had not settled down to careers yet but had only minor financial problems. However, the other son was generally in financial difficulties – largely of his own making.

John wanted to be fair to all his boys, but was not happy with the idea of just sharing out his assets between them. They did not all have the same need, and the youngest son in particular would be likely to squander any inheritance. John wanted a solution which would ensure that help was available to all his sons if they needed it but would protect the assets otherwise. He decided to set up a discretionary trust in favour of all the sons. He appointed his own two brothers (the sons' uncles) as trustees and gave them discretion to make payments and loans from the trust fund to the sons if or when, in the trustees' opinion, such help was warranted. After ten years (by which time John felt the boys should all take responsibility for themselves), the remaining trust assets were to be distributed equally between them.

Accumulation and maintenance trusts

There are a number of special types of discretionary trust and one of the most important, from the point of view of families, is the accumulation and maintenance trust. Because of the tax treatment this is a very popular device for making gifts to, or for the benefit of, children. The trust may be in favour of either named beneficiaries – for example, 'my daughters, Kate and Anna' or a class of beneficiaries such as 'my grandchildren'.

Special rules apply to accumulation and maintenance trusts: in particular, one or more of the beneficiaries *must* become entitled to either income or capital from the trust on or before the age of 25. Provided this rule is met, there is the scope for great flexibility over when other beneficiaries start to benefit. In the run up to the entitlement coming into effect, no beneficiary may have any interest in possession. Instead, income from the assets must be accumulated within the trust fund, though it can be paid out to pay for the maintenance, education or other benefit of one or more of the beneficiaries. Income and capital do not have to be paid out at the same time or to the same beneficiaries: for example, one child might start to receive an income at age 25 and another might have the right to all the capital at some later date.

There is a limit on how long the trust can exist. The period is either 25 years, or longer if all the beneficiaries have a common grandparent (in other words, if the beneficiaries are brothers, sisters or first cousins; illegitimate and adopted children are treated in the same way as legitimate ones).

Although a trust may be for the benefit of a group of beneficiaries, such as all your grandchildren, there must be at least one living beneficiary at the time the trust is set up. (But, if there is only one and that beneficiary subsequently dies, the trust can still carry on.)

EXAMPLE 9.3

David set up a trust to accept a gift for his first granddaughter, Jemima. Bearing in mind that there might be more grandchildren to come, he established an accumulation and maintenance trust in favour of all his grandchildren. For the present, he has settled £5,000 in the trust, but can add more later if he wishes. Jemima is to become entitled to a lump sum from the trust when she reaches age 25. In the meantime, money can be paid out – to pay for school fees, say – at the discretion of the trustees, who are David and his wife, Ruth.

Other special types of discretionary trust

Accumulation and maintenance trusts are just one type of 'special trust'. There are others which also benefit from favourable tax treatment. Most are outside the scope of gift planning (they include, *inter alia*, pension schemes, personal pension plans, compensation funds and unit trusts), but two may be of use:

1. *Charitable trusts*   If you want to give large amounts to a range of charities, setting up your own charitable trust is an option worth considering (see p. 38).
2. *Disabled trusts*   For assets placed in trust on or after 10 March 1981, mainly for the benefit of someone who is incapable of looking after their own property because of mental disorder, or someone who is receiving attendance allowance, the disabled person is treated as if they have an interest in possession. This means that the interest in possession tax rules apply rather than those for discretionary trusts (see below).

Taxation of trusts

The tax treatment of trusts is crucial to any decision regarding the use of a trust as a way of making gifts. Unfortunately, it is also complex. The government has proposed changes to simplify the income and capital taxation of trusts and to bring it into harmony with the personal tax regime;[31] these proposals are briefly summarised at the end of each section below. The IHT position of trusts has been overhauled in recent years and no further changes are expected.

Interest in possession trusts

Putting a gift in trust

If you make a gift which is placed in an interest in possession trust, you are treated as if you had made a potentially exempt transfer (PET). So there will be no IHT charge provided you survive for seven years after making the gift (see pp. 79–81 for more details). If you die within seven years, the trustees will normally be liable for the tax due. No special rules apply in respect of CGT, so check the ordinary rules to see if tax will be payable (see Chapters 5 and 6).

The trust's tax position

The trust will receive income from investing the trust assets either as gross income, with basic rate income tax already deducted, or, if dividend income, with tax at 20 per cent deducted. The trustees must pay basic rate tax of 25 per cent (in 1994–95) on any gross income. The trust does not have an allowance to set against income tax and does not pay income tax at the higher rate however large the income.

The trust will be liable for CGT on capital gains at the basic rate of 25 per cent (in 1994–95). The first slice of capital gains is tax-free. The tax-free slice for the trust is half that available to individuals and is £2,900 for the 1994–95 tax year.

Payments to beneficiaries

Income paid from the trust to beneficiaries is net of basic rate income tax but accompanied by a tax credit. If you are a non-taxpayer, or pay tax at 20 per cent, you can reclaim all or part of the tax. Higher rate taxpayers have extra to pay on the grossed-up amount. There may instead be an arrangement for income to be paid direct to beneficiaries. In the case of dividends paid this way, the tax credit is only 20 per cent – non-taxpayers can reclaim the tax, 20 per cent and basic rate taxpayers have no further tax to pay, and higher rate

---

[31]Inland Revenue. 1991. *Trusts*, a consultative document. London, Inland Revenue.

taxpayers must pay extra.

If you receive payment of capital from the trust, there is no CGT for you to pay and you cannot reclaim any CGT paid by the trust.

When the interest in possession ends.

If you have an interest in possession, you are treated, for tax purposes, as owning the assets in the trust – the reversionary interest is ignored. If there is more than one beneficiary, you are treated as owning the trust assets in proportion to your shares in the income from them. When your interest in possession ends, you are deemed to make a gift of the assets to the beneficiary with the reversionary interest. Provided you are 'giving' the assets to an individual or to an appropriate type of trust, the gift counts as a PET and no tax is payable provided you survive seven years (see pp. 79–81). If the assets pass, say, to a discretionary trust, the gift counts as chargeable and there may be an immediate IHT bill, depending on your running total of gifts during the last seven years (pp. 74–77).

If, when the trust ends, you become entitled to receive the trust property outright, there is no IHT liability.

If a beneficiary's interest in possession ends during his or her lifetime, the beneficiary is deemed to be disposing of the trust assets and there may be CGT to pay. There is no CGT liability when a life interest ends on the death of the beneficiary holding the interest.

A reversionary interest in an interest in possession trust counts as 'excluded property' for the IHT purposes, which means that it is completely outside the IHT net. This can be useful, a gift of a reversionary interest cannot create an IHT bill (see Example 9.4).

EXAMPLE 9.4

When Charlie died, he left most of his assets (some £200,000 in total) in trust, giving his wife, Molly, a life interest in the income from the trust and his daughter, Pru, the reversionary interest in the trust property. Pru is in her thirties and has children of her own. Her husband has a well-paid job and the family is financially comfortable. Pru would prefer that her father's assets passed to her children. So she decides to release her reversionary interest in the trust and give it to the children. There is no IHT to pay, because reversionary interests are excluded from the IHT regime.

Proposed changes

No changes are proposed to the way income tax is charged in respect of an interest in possession trust. However, the Inland Revenue have suggested that it is anomalous for the trust's capital gains to be taxed only at the basic rate even if the beneficiary is taxed on income and gains at the higher rate of 40 per cent (in 1994–95), and that the taxation of gains for this type of trust should be the same as whatever system is adopted for discretionary trusts.

Discretionary trusts

Putting a gift into trust

A gift put into a discretionary trust counts as a chargeable gift for IHT and can create an immediate tax bill (see p. 73). Whether or not you have to pay any tax depends on whether you can claim an exemption (for example, the yearly tax-free slice of £3,000) or, if not, on your running total of chargeable gifts during the previous seven years.

There may be CGT due on the gift, if you are giving assets other than cash, but you can claim hold-over relief (see p. 70).

The trust's tax position

There is a 'periodic charge' for IHT on the value of the trust property. This charge is made on the tenth anniversary of the setting up of the trust and at 10-year intervals after that. The amount of tax due is worked out as follows:

- *Add* up the value of the trust at the time of the tax charge *and* any gifts made by the settlor (i.e. the person who set up the discretionary trust) to other trusts (apart from charitable trusts) set up on the same day at their value on that day. To this, *add* the value of chargeable gifts made by the settlor in the seven years up to the date of the trust starting.
- Work out the tax due on that total amount by *deducting* the tax-free slice and *multiplying* by 20 per cent (in the 1994–95 tax year).
- *Divide* the tax due by the value of everything owned by the discretionary trust. This gives you the 'effective rate of tax'.
- Take 30 per cent of the effective rate (i.e. *multiply* by 0.3). This gives you the rate at which tax will be charged on the trust property.

This means that the *highest* rate of tax that will have to be paid is 30 per cent of the lifetime rate of 20 per cent – that is, 6 per cent – and the rate could be as low as nothing at all.

EXAMPLE 9.5

Peter set up a discretionary trust on 1 June 1984, paying £60,000 into it. That day, he also set up an interest in possession trust in favour of his daughter and paid £50,000 into that. His cumulative total of chargeable gifts over the seven years before 1 June 1984 was £20,000.

On 1 June 1994, the first 10-year IHT charge becomes payable on the discretionary trust which is now valued at £180,000. The tax due is worked out as follows:

Current value of discretionary trust	£180,000
plus original value of other trust set up on 1 June 1984	£50,000
plus Peter's seven-year running total up to 31 May 1984	£20,000
	£250,000
less tax-free slice	£150,000
	£100,000
Tax @ 20% on £100,000	£20,000
Effective rate of tax (£20,000 ÷ £180,000)	11.111%
30% × effective rate	3.333%
IHT due on the trust (3.333% × £180,000)	£6,000

If money or assets are paid out of a discretionary trust, an 'interim charge' for IHT is made and must be paid by the trustees. The charge is worked out by multiplying the full 10-year charges by 1/40 for each three-month period during which the property was in the trust since the last periodic charge to IHT. (The procedure is slightly different for payments made before the first 10-year period is up.) This interim charge is also called an 'exit charge'. The tax charge is scaled down similarly in the case of property added to the trust after the start of the relevant 10-year period.

The trustees are also responsible for paying income tax on income received by the trust. Income tax is charged at the basic rate (25% for 1994–95) plus an additional rate of 10 per cent – that is, at a rate of 35 per cent.[32] Tax credits are set against the tax due. For example, on dividend income which comes with a tax credit of 20 per cent, tax at a further 15 per cent is payable. CGT on any taxable capital gains is also payable by the trustees at 35 per cent, though the trust can set a tax-free allowance of £2,900 against the first slice of gains.

Payments to beneficiaries

Income is paid out to beneficiaries net of tax at 35 per cent (see above) but with a tax credit for the tax paid. As a beneficiary, you are responsible for income tax on the 'grossed up' value of income you receive – that is, the actual income plus the tax credit – and you set the tax credit against your personal tax bill. This means that if you are a basic-rate taxpayer, 20 per cent taxpayer or non-taxpayer you will get back the excess tax paid.

If you receive a payment of capital from the trust, there is no CGT for you to pay and you cannot reclaim any CGT paid by the trust. Note that once income has been accumulated within the trust, the payment of it to a beneficiary will normally count as a payment of capital.

When the trust ends

When the discretionary trust comes to an end, an 'exit' charge is made on the whole of the trust property as if it were any other payment from the trust (see above).

Proposed changes

The current 35 per cent charge on a discretionary trust's income is a compromise between the lower basic rate of tax and the higher 40 per cent rate which apply to individuals. A compromise is needed because, at the time income arises within the trust, it is not known who the ultimate beneficiary of it will be or what his/her tax position is. However, the Inland Revenue has suggested that this

---

[32] Though note that the additional rate is charged on *net* trust income (i.e. income less any allowable expenses incurred by the trust).

higher charge may be too high in the case of small trusts where beneficiaries are less likely to be higher rate taxpayers, and may be inappropriate in the case of income which is paid out immediately to beneficiaries where experience tells the Revenue that the excess tax is often reclaimed.

The Revenue poses the questions: whether the income of small trusts should be charged only at the basic rate; whether the additional charge should be levied only on income that is not immediately distributed and only on income to be accumulated above a specified threshold (i.e. above a basic rate band); and whether the additional charge should be raised from 10 per cent to 15 per cent to bring it into line with personal tax rates?

There are similar considerations in the case CGT.

Accumulation and maintenance trusts

Putting a gift into trust

Although accumulation and maintenance trusts are a special form of discretionary trust, the tax rules are much more favourable. A payment into an accumulation and maintenance trust counts as a PET (see p. 57) and so there is no tax to pay provided you survive for seven years after making the gift.

Normal CGT rules apply to a gift to an accumulation and maintenance trust, so you will need to check whether there is any CGT to pay (see Chapter 6).

The trust's tax position

An accumulation and maintenance trust is not subject to the periodic charge regime – that is, there is no IHT to pay on the value of the trust during the lifetime of the trust nor is there any IHT charge when payments are made to beneficiaries.

The trustees are responsible for paying income tax on income received by the trust at a rate of 35 per cent (as for other discretionary trusts, see above). They are also liable for CGT on taxable gains at 35 per cent, but can make up to £2,900 worth of gains tax free.

Payments to beneficiaries

The rules are the same as for other discretionary trusts (see previous page).

When the trust ends

There is no IHT charge. The trustees may need to pay CGT on any capital gains – this cannot be reclaimed by the beneficiaries. Amounts received by beneficiaries are treated as under 'Payments to beneficiaries' on p. 105.

Proposed changes

The changes discussed by the Inland Revenue in respect of discretionary trusts (see p. 105) apply also to accumulation and maintenance trusts.

Tax points to watch out for

If you, or your husband or wife, set up a trust and your own child or children (under age 18 and unmarried) receive income from it, that income will count as yours and you will be liable for tax on it at your highest tax rate. If your children receive capital payments from such a trust, these payments will also count as your *income* to the extent that they can be matched against income received by the trust and accumulated for the child (or children).

If you set up a trust and your husband or wife is a beneficiary, or potential beneficiary, under it, the income and gains made by the trust are usually treated as if they are yours, not the trust's, and you will have to account for tax due on them.

PART 3

INHERITANCE

CHAPTER **10**

MAKING A WILL

WILLS ARE IMPORTANT

'Now, Mr Hope,' the solicitor's face became even more serious, 'I take it you have made a will?'

'Well, no,' replied Richard, 'but my affairs are very straightforward. Everything would go to my wife – after all, she'd have the children to look after.'

'Precisely, Mr Hope. Without a will, only part of your estate would pass to your wife. Although your children would also benefit, I'm afraid your wife might need to sell the home and there would certainly be a number of unnecessary costs. I would strongly advise you to make a will.'

A will is a legal document which says how your possessions (your *estate*) are to be dealt with when you die. Even if your estate is small and your intentions regarding it extremely simple, you should still make a will. If you do not, a number of problems can arise, as follows:

- Your survivors may waste time trying to find out whether or not you did write a will; it may take them a long time to trace all your possessions; and they may have to spend time and money tracing relatives.

- If there is no will, it may take longer and cost more to 'prove' the estate (an administrative process which has to be completed before your estate can be 'distributed' – that is, handed on – to your heirs).

- Without a will, your next of kin (who will often be a wife or husband) will usually be appointed to sort out your affairs. At a time of bereavement, they may prefer not to take on this role and you may, in any case, have friends or relatives who would be more suited to the task.
- The law will dictate how your estate is passed on and this may not coincide with your wishes.
- The law may require that various trusts are set up with the trust assets invested in particular ways. The terms of these trusts may be overly restrictive and, especially where small sums are involved, unnecessarily large expenses may be incurred.
- Your heirs may have to pay inheritance tax (or more tax) than would have been the case had you used your will to pass on your possessions tax-efficiently (see Chapter 12).

Apart from avoiding these problems and ensuring that your possessions are given away as you would choose, a will can be used for other purposes too: you can appoint guardians to care for young children; and you can express your preferences about funeral arrangements and any wishes about the use of your body for medical purposes after death.

Note that the rules relating to wills and intestacy in Scotland differ in a number of respects from the rules for the rest of the United Kingdom. The rules described in this chapter apply to England and Wales.

A few definitions

There are three main types of player involved in a will, as follows:

1. *Testator/testatrix*   The man or woman whose will it is. You must be aged 18 or over (and be of sound mind) to make a valid will.
2. *Beneficiary*   A person or organisation who is left something (in other words 'benefits') under a will.
3. *Personal representative*   The person, people, or organisation who sees that your estate is distributed following your death. If you have not made a will, they are called your *administrator* and they will distribute your estate in accordance with the law. If you have made a will, they are called your *executor* and they will try to ensure that the instructions in your will are carried out.

Dying without a will

If you die without making a will (called dying 'intestate') the law dictates how your estate will be passed on. The law aims, in the first instance, to protect your immediate family – husband or wife, and children. This might coincide with your wishes but, even if it did, it still might not result in your estate being used as you had expected or would have wished. Furthermore, dependants who are not formally part of your family – for example, an unmarried partner – have no automatic rights under the intestacy laws (though they might still have a claim against your estate – see p. 123).

The intestacy laws assume that all your possessions could be sold by your personal representative to convert your whole estate into cash which would then be distributed according to the rules described below. In practice, the possessions would not necessarily be sold and could be passed on intact, but problems can arise where there is a large possession – for example, the family home – if it needs to be split between two or more beneficiaries. The intestacy laws operate as follows.

If you are survived by a husband or wife and no children

Your husband or wife is entitled to all your *personal chattels* (i.e. personal possessions, such as clothes, furniture, jewellery, private cars and so on). If your estate is valued at £200,000 or less, your husband or wife also inherits the whole estate. (See Chapter 11 for guidance on valuing your estate.)

If your estate is valued at more than £200,000, your husband or wife gets the whole lot, provided you had no living parents or brothers or sisters at the time of your death. If you are survived by parents, brothers or sisters, your husband or wife is entitled to a fixed sum of £200,000 (plus interest at a set rate from the date of death until the date the payment is made) plus half of whatever remains. The remainder goes to your parents or, if they are dead, to your brothers and sisters. Chart 10.1 summarises the position.

Chart 10.1 Who inherits if you leave a husband/wife and no children

Is your estate worth more than £200,000?	→	NO →	Husband/wife inherits whole estate
↓ YES ↓			
Do you have parents? ↓ NO ↓	→	YES →	Husband/wife gets £200,000 (with interest) plus half the remaining estate. Your parents inherit the rest.
Do you have brothers or sisters? ↓ NO ↓	→	YES →	Husband/wife gets £200,000 (with interest) plus half the remaining estate. Your brothers and sisters (or their children) share the rest.
Husband/wife inherits whole estate			

EXAMPLE 10.1

Jeremy and Ali had been married for ten years when tragically Jeremy died in a road accident. He was only 36 and, though he had several times thought about making a will, he had not got around to doing it. His estate was valued at £250,000 and he would have left everything to Ali, but under the intestacy laws the estate was divided between Ali and his parents as follows:

Ali's share:

Fixed sum	£200,000
plus interest	£4,940
plus half the remaining estate (i.e. £250,000 –£204,940)	£22,530
Total	£227,470
Jeremy's parents' share	£22,530

If you are survived by children

If you leave children, but no husband or wife, the inheritance position is simple: your children share your estate equally. Note that 'children' includes offspring from your most recent marriage (if applicable), any previous marriages, adopted children and illegitimate children. However, it does not include stepchildren.

If you are survived by a husband or wife, he/she is entitled to all your personal possessions. And, if your estate is valued at £125,000 or less, he/she also inherits the whole of that.

If your estate is valued at more than £125,000, your husband or wife receives a fixed sum of £125,000 (plus interest at a set rate from the date of death until the date payment is made) and a life interest in half of the remaining estate. A life interest gives him/her the right to the income from that part of the estate (or use of it in the case of, say, a house), but he/she cannot touch the capital. (Note that the husband or wife can decide to take an appropriately calculated lump sum from the estate in place of a life interest.) The rest of the estate passes to your children to be shared equally between them. They also become entitled to the capital bearing the life interest when your husband or wife dies. (Note that children can only inherit capital outright once they reach the age of 18, so they have an income entitlement up to that age.) Chart 10.2 summarises the position.

Chart 10.2 Who inherits if you leave children

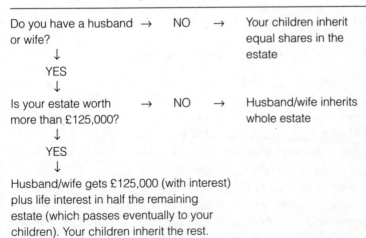

Do you have a husband → NO → Your children inherit
or wife? equal shares in the
↓ estate
YES
↓

Is your estate worth → NO → Husband/wife inherits
more than £125,000? whole estate
↓
YES
↓

Husband/wife gets £125,000 (with interest)
plus life interest in half the remaining
estate (which passes eventually to your
children). Your children inherit the rest.

EXAMPLE 10.2

Alan died leaving an estate valued at £250,000. Of this amount £200,000 represented his half-share in the family home. However, he had made no will. Under the intestacy rules, his wife, Julia, and his only child inherited the estate in the following shares:

Julia's share:

Capital: fixed sum	£125,000
plus interest	£3,090
Total capital	£128,090
plus income/use from £60,955	

Child's share:

Capital now	£60,955
Capital to be set aside for future	£60,955

Unfortunately, Julia's outright inheritance of £128,090 and interest in a further £60,955 come to less than the value of the family home. In order to comply with the intestacy rules requiring capital of £121,910 in total to be set aside for the child, part of the family home must be held in trust for the child.

If you are survived by no near relatives

If you leave no husband or wife and no children, the intestacy rules rank your heirs in the order in which they will inherit your estate. Chart 10.3 shows how this works.

If you have no relatives who are eligible to inherit (see Chart 10.3), your estate passes to the Crown in *bona vacantia* (which literally means 'unclaimed goods'). The Crown may make ex gratia payments if your dependants or relatives make an application to it. It is important to realise that claimants have no *right* to receive anything – payments are at the discretion of the Crown. Applicants who are most likely to succeed include the following:

- Someone who had a long, close association with you: for example, an unmarried partner or someone who lived with you as a child.
- Someone who you clearly intended to benefit under a will that was invalid for some reason.

Chart 10.3   Who inherits if you leave no near relatives

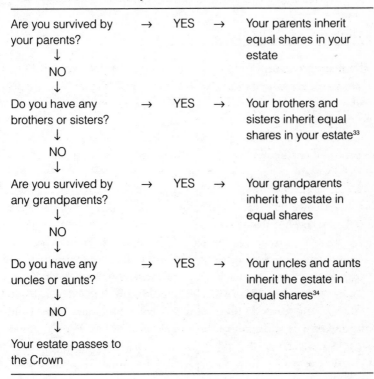

Are you survived by → YES → Your parents inherit
your parents?   equal shares in your
     ↓   estate
    NO
     ↓

Do you have any → YES → Your brothers and
brothers or sisters?   sisters inherit equal
     ↓   shares in your estate[33]
    NO
     ↓

Are you survived by → YES → Your grandparents
any grandparents?   inherit the estate in
     ↓   equal shares
    NO
     ↓

Do you have any → YES → Your uncles and aunts
uncles or aunts?   inherit the estate in
     ↓   equal shares[34]
    NO
     ↓

Your estate passes to
the Crown

EXAMPLE 10.3

Harold died aged 89. He was an only child. His wife and parents died before him and he himself had no children. But his Uncle Jack (who died long ago) had two children, Jean and Richard, who are both still living. They each inherit half of Harold's estate.

---

[33]If a brother or sister has died before you, their offspring, if any, inherit instead. If you have no full brothers or sisters, any half-brothers or half-sisters will share the estate instead.

[34]If any uncle or aunt has died before you, their offspring inherit instead. If you have no full uncles or aunts, any half-uncles or half-aunts share the estate instead.

Partial intestacy

Your will should cover all your assets. If you do not specify how part of your estate is to be used, that part will be subject to the intestacy rules even though the rest of your estate is disposed of in accordance with the will.

Problems caused by intestacy

The main problems of intestacy arise where you are survived by a partner (either married or not) and/or you have children. Unless you make a will, you cannot be certain that they will be adequately provided for in the event of your death.

If you are not married to your partner, he/she has no automatic right of inheritance in the event of your death. If your partner can prove that he/she was partly or wholly maintained by you when you were alive, he/she may be able to claim a share of your estate under the Inheritance (Provision for Family and Dependants) Act 1975 (see later). But, even if the claim is successful, the procedure may take a long time and could be costly (see p. 123). The government has said that it intends to change the law to make it easier for unmarried partners to claim 'reasonable financial provision' from a deceased partner's estate. No date has yet been set for this change.

If you are married, there is a tendency to assume that your husband or wife will automatically inherit everything. The foregoing sections have shown that this is by no means certain. And, even if you are happy for your husband or wife and children to share your assets, the practical application of the intestacy rules may be very distressing to your survivors. Where the estate must be shared between husband or wife and children, or husband or wife and other relatives, your husband or wife has the right to claim the family home as part or all of his/her inheritance (provided he/she lived there with you prior to your death). If the home is worth more than the amount he/she is entitled to inherit, your husband or wife can 'buy' the excess from the estate. But if he/she does not have sufficient resources to be able to do this, the home may have to be sold so that the cash raised can be split as required by the intestacy provisions.

The intestacy laws are very rigid concerning the inheritance of assets by children. The assets must usually be converted to cash and placed in trust where they are to be invested in a restricted range of 'safe' assets. This can cause a number of problems: first, it may be more desirable to keep the assets rather than convert them to cash; secondly, the amount involved may really be so small that setting up a trust may be disproportionately expensive. The yield on the 'safe' investments will tend to be lower than is required to keep pace with inflation and generally lower than the return available on many other investments – this can result in an inadequate income for a husband or wife who has a lifetime interest in the income from the assets.

Drawing up a will

In many people's minds, making a will is inextricably linked with using a solicitor, but this need not be so. Provided your personal circumstances are not overly complicated and you understand what you are doing, there is no reason why you should not write your own will. There are a number of books and kits available to help you do this: for example, Consumers' Association's *Wills and Probate* or *Make Your Will* Action Pack.[35] The main advantage of writing your own will is, of course, the saving in solicitors' fees. For a simple will – for example, involving only assets in the United Kingdom and leaving everything to your husband or wife – many solicitors would charge around £50 or so. However, you could pay double this for a more complicated will, depending on the time spent on it.

A will, to fulfil its purpose, must record your intentions clearly and unambiguously and should include contingency plans to cover the possibility, for example, of a beneficiary dying before you. There are also various pitfalls to be avoided – some that would invalidate the will and leave your estate subject to the intestacy laws, and others which would not invalidate the will but would interfere with the intentions expressed in it. For example, a valid will must be signed by two or more witnesses, who may not also be beneficiaries under the will; so, if you are leaving anything to your husband or wife, say, do not ask him/her to be a witness – the will would be valid, but your spouse would not be allowed to inherit under it. A solicitor should be competent at drawing up a will for you which meets your own

[35]Available from Consumers' Association, Castlemead, Gascoyne Way, Hertford X, SG14 1LH or Freephone 0800 252100 to order on Access/Visa.

and the legal requirements, and should be able to advise on how best to leave your assets. Unfortunately, using a solicitor is not always a guarantee of quality: in a sample of wills assessed by experts for *Which?* magazine, out of twenty-one wills only five were considered good, and most 'could have been improved'. However, only one was considered 'disastrous'.[36]

There are also a growing number of will-writing services. These are often small firms working under a franchise or as agents of a larger company. Most work by gathering the necessary details from you and feeding these into a computer which produces your will. Unlike solicitors, people running, or working for, will-writing firms are not required to have any formal legal qualifications, though they will probably have received some initial training and the computer software they are using will have been developed using legal experts; these firms may use a solicitor to draw up complicated wills. Will-writing services usually charge a fixed fee (set in advance) of around £50; some services charge less. Unfortunately, there have been problems with some of these services in the past: a number of firms have gone bust and, in one case, it was found that a potentially large number of the wills written contained a flaw and might not be valid. In October 1991, The Institute of Professional Will Writers was established to set and enforce minimum standards amongst its members – membership is voluntary and not industry-wide.

Renewing your will

You should not view making a will as a task once done to be forgotten. As your circumstances alter, so your will needs to be updated. In some situations – for example, if you marry or remarry – any will made before the marriage will automatically be invalidated (unless it was a will made specifically in contemplation of the marriage). A will is also automatically revoked by divorce, but the same is not true of separation – in that situation, you should review the terms of your will. Other circumstances in which you might want to revise your will are the birth or adoption of a child, or if you decide that you would like to leave a legacy to a charity. It is wise to read through your will every two years, say, as a matter of course, to check that it reflects your current wishes. If you do decide to alter a

---

[36] 'Making your will' in *Which?*, Consumers' Association, June 1991, p. 316.

will – even slightly – it is better to draw up a new will containing the revisions than to add an amendment (a 'codicil'). The trouble with codicils is that they can easily become detached from the will and lost. A new will should always start with a clause revoking any previous wills; this automatically invalidates any earlier wills. (Interestingly, if a will is not automatically revoked – by, say, a later will or marriage – the law requires that you *physically* destroy your will if it is to be revoked. Simply putting a cross through it and scribbling 'cancelled' or 'revoked' across it would not be enough.)

Making gifts in your will

In your will, you can give away anything you own. There are different types of gift and the distinction between them is important both for tax reasons (see Chapter 11) and because of the order in which they can be redirected to meet expenses and settle debts that you leave at the time of your death. The main types of gift are described as follows.

Specific gift

This can be a named or identifiable possession such as a piece of furniture, an item of jewellery or a particular car. It may be a specific possession that you own *at the time you write the will*; if you later sell the item the beneficiary who was to have received it will get nothing after all.

Alternatively, you might leave a more general type of specific gift. This would be the gift of a possession but not restricted to a specific item that you own at the time of drawing up the will. For example, you might give away 'the car I own at the time of my death', which would take into account the possibility that you might change your car from time to time.

A specific gift might be even more widely defined: for example, simply 'a car'. In this latter case, the executors of your will would have a duty to make sure that the beneficiary received a car – either one that you owned at the time of death or, if you had none, one bought specifically to fulfil the terms of the will – or, alternatively, the trustees would have to pay over an equivalent sum of money.

Legacies

A 'pecuniary legacy' is a particular type of specific gift which is a straightforward gift of money: for example, '£1,000 to my niece, Claire'.

A 'demonstrative legacy' can be either a general gift or a pecuniary legacy which is to be paid from a specific fund: for example, 'a violin to be paid for out of my account with Barclays Bank' or '£1,000 from my account with the Halifax Building Society'. If there was not enough money in the account, the shortfall would have to be met by using other assets in the estate.

Residuary gift

A will which assigned every part of your estate as a particular gift or legacy would be out of date almost immediately, because the value of your estate fluctuates even in the course of your daily transactions and will alter more widely during the course of time. Therefore, it is usual to leave whatever remains of your estate, after all your debts, expenses and various gifts as listed above have been paid, as a 'residuary gift' or 'residue'. You may intend your residue to be a substantial gift, or it may be a small amount with, say, the bulk of your estate given away through pecuniary gifts.

To meet debts and expenses, any intestate part of your estate will be used up first, followed by the residue.

EXAMPLE 10.4

Daisy (see p. 51) died at the ripe old age of 92. Her sole survivor, Albert, had expected to inherit a sizeable sum. However, Daisy had already given Hadley Hall to Albert and clearly considered that was enough, because out of the £750,000 estate that she left, she gave £600,000 to a spread of charities. After deducting outstanding debts, funeral expenses and a very small tax bill, Albert inherited the residue of only £20,000.

Gifts you do not want to make

By omission, your will can also express your intention not to leave anything (or only very little) to people who might have expected to inherit from you. However, if these people were dependent on you, they have the right to make a claim through the courts under the Inheritance (Provision for Family and Dependants) Act 1975 for reasonable provision out of your estate. The main people who are entitled to make such a claim are as follows:

- Your husband or wife.
- A former husband or wife, provided he/she has not remarried (and is not precluded from making a claim under the divorce settlement).
- A child of yours (whether legitimate, illegitimate or adopted).
- A child of your family (i.e. a stepchild or foster child).
- An unmarried partner.

An application under the Act must usually be made within six months of the personal representatives being given permission to dispose of the estate, though the court can extend this time limit. The court decides whether or not the applicant is entitled to financial support from the estate and, if it decides in favour of the applicant, it can order the payment of either a lump sum or income (or both).

You might seek to anticipate and thwart such a claim by giving away as much of your estate as possible, but this strategy will not work, because the court has the power to revoke such gifts in order to ensure that enough funds are available to meet the needs of your surviving dependants.

You can include in your will a statement setting out your reasons for excluding your dependants and the court will take this into account. It would be worth seeking advice from a solicitor about the most effective wording to use.

CHAPTER 11

TAX AT THE TIME OF DEATH

NOT JUST A RICH MAN'S TAX

'When I die, my will is very simple,' said Percy, draining his glass. 'I haven't so very much to leave behind, but I'll give my son a bit to help him with his business. Then, I'll just split what's left between the wife and Rose.'

'You should watch out,' replied his friend as he rose to buy another round. 'If there is any tax to pay, it will probably come out of Rose's share – she might end up with a lot less than you're hoping.'

When you die, you are deemed to make a gift of all your possessions just before death. There is no capital gains tax (CGT) on your estate, but there may be extra tax due on gifts which you had made in the seven years before death.

Tax on gifts made before death

Chapter 7 looked at the immediate tax position of gifts made during your lifetime. In the case of potentially exempt transfers (PETs) there was no tax to pay at the time of the gift, but if you die within seven years of making a PET, the gift becomes a 'chargeable transfer' and tax is due. The rate of tax ranges from 8 per cent up to 40 per cent, depending on the time that has elapsed since you originally made the gift (see p. 80).

Similarly, a chargeable transfer – on which tax may have been paid at the time of the gift but at the lower lifetime IHT rate of 20 per cent – will be reassessed and there may be further tax to pay if you die within seven years of making the gift (see p. 78).

The tax due on the PET or chargeable transfer is based on the amount of the running total of all chargeable gifts made by you in the seven years up to the time of the gift. Gifts which were formally PETs may, following the death, be reassessed as chargeable transfers, so the running total for any particular gift may be revised upwards and thus be greater than it had been at the time the gift was made.

Tax due on earlier gifts as the result of death is the liability of the person to whom you made the gift, but if they cannot or will not pay, the tax will be recovered from your estate. If the estate pays the tax, this will itself count as a gift on which tax will be due.

There is some tax relief if the value of a PET or chargeable transfer has fallen since the time it was first made; whoever is paying the tax is allowed to deduct the fall in value from the original value of the gift. Bear in mind, however, that the original value of a gift was the loss to the giver *not* the value to the recipient, so even a large percentage fall in the value of the item in the recipient's hands may have only a small impact on the value of the item for IHT purposes (see Example 11.1). The fall-in-value relief is not given automatically; the person paying the tax must make a claim to the Capital Taxes Office (see Useful addresses).

EXAMPLE 11.1

In September 1990, Dorothy gave her niece, Charlotte, one of a pair of rare antique vases. As a pair, the vases had a market price of £110,000, but individually they were each worth only £40,000. The value of the gift was the loss to Dorothy, in other words, the difference between the market price of the pair and the price of the remaining vase: £110,00 – £40,000 = £70,000. The gift counted as a potentially exempt transfer and so there was no tax to pay.

In August 1993, Dorothy died and Charlotte received a demand for tax on the gift of the vase. She had the vase valued by a local dealer who put a market price of only £35,000 on the vase now. Charlotte agreed to the reduced value of the gift which was worked out as the original loss to the giver less the fall in value: £70,000 – £5,000 = £65,000.

Tax now due on the gift is calculated as follows. Just before she made the gift to Charlotte, in September 1990, Dorothy's cumulative total of gifts, including other PETs that have become chargeable since her death, came to £162,000 – more than the tax-free slice at 1993–94 tax rates, so tax is due on the gift of the vase. Less than three years have passed since Dorothy made the gift, so the full death rate of 40 per cent applies. The IHT payable is thus: 40% × £65,000 = £26,000. Charlotte agrees to pay this.

Tax on your estate

On your death, IHT is due on the value of your estate (plus certain gifts made before death) if it comes to more than the tax-free slice. The tax-free slice is generally increased each year in line with inflation, however, for the 1992–93 tax year, it was uprated by slightly more than this to £150,000 and has been kept at that level for 1993–94 and 1994–95. (See Appendix on p. 155 for previous years' figures.) This may seem a large sum, but £150,000 can soon be swallowed up, especially if you own your own home. Your estate is made up of:

- the value of all your possessions at the time of death, including your home, car, personal belongings, cash, investments, and so on,
- *plus* any gifts with reservation (see p. 81) that you made,
- *plus* the proceeds of any insurance policies which are paid to your estate,
- *less* your debts,
- *less* reasonable funeral expenses.

This total is called your 'free estate' and it is the amount that is available for giving away. For the purpose of calculating any IHT, you can deduct from the free estate any gifts made in your will that count as tax-free gifts (see below). But you must *add* all the PETs and other taxable gifts which you made in the seven years before death to find the relevant running total (see p. 74). If the running total comes to more than the tax-free slice, inheritance tax at a rate of 40 per cent is payable.

Gifts under your will

If the value of your estate plus taxable gifts in the seven years before death comes to less than the tax-free slice of £150,000, making gifts under your will is fairly straightforward: assuming that the estate is sufficiently large (after paying off debts and expenses), the recipients will receive the amounts that you specify in your will.

However, if there is inheritance tax due on the estate, matters are not always so simple. To work out how much the recipients will actually receive, you need to know how tax will be allocated between the various gifts. For IHT purposes, there are three types of gift which you can leave in a will:

1. *Tax-free gifts* (see above and Chapter 5)   There is no tax at all on these.
2. *Free-of-tax-gifts* (not to be confused with tax-free gifts)   The recipient gets the amount you specify and any tax due is paid out of the residue of the estate.
3. *Gifts which bear their own tax*   With these, the amount you give is treated as a gross gift *out of which* the recipient must pay any tax due.

In general, a specific gift under your will is automatically treated as a free-of-tax gift unless it is tax-free or you have explicitly stated that the gift should bear its own tax. To avoid confusion, it is a good idea to state for every gift whether it is 'free-of-tax' or 'to bear its own tax'.

Whatever is left of your estate after deducting specific gifts is called the 'residue' or 'residual gift'. The residue can be either a tax-free gift or taxable in which case it bears its own tax. The residue may be split, with part counting as a tax-free gift and part as a taxable one.

The fun starts when you try to calculate how much tax will be deducted either from the residue of the estate or from the specific gifts. The calculations vary depending on the mix of gifts which you are making. The following sections describe the main possibilities.

If you find the calculations that follow daunting, do not despair – you can ask your solicitor or accountant to work out for you the tax position of various gifts that you are considering as part of your will. The most important point is that you should at least be aware that tax can affect the gifts in different ways.

If all your gifts are tax-free

This is the simplest case. As with lifetime gifts, some gifts from your estate are free of IHT, in particular: gifts of any amount to your husband or wife, gifts to charities, gifts for the public benefit, gifts to political parties and gifts to Housing Associations (see pp. 53–54 for more details).

So, for example, you might make a gift to charity and leave the residue to your husband or wife. Since both types of gift are tax-free, there is no inheritance tax at all.

EXAMPLE 11.2

When Connie dies in May 1994, she leaves an estate made up as follows:

Cottage	£65,000
Personal possessions	£21,500
Cash in bank	£496
Investments	£331,204
Gross value of estate	£418,200
less various small debts	£500
less funeral expenses, administration costs, etc.	£2,700
Net value of 'free estate'	£415,000

Connie had made no gifts during the previous seven years. Since the value of the estate exceeds the tax-free slice, you might expect IHT to have been payable, but in fact it was not because Connie used the whole of the 'free estate' to make tax-free gifts. She left a legacy of £100,000 to charity and the residue to her husband.

If all your specific gifts bear their own tax

Again, this is a relatively simple case. The amount of tax on each gift is in proportion to the values of chargeable gifts. This is done by working out the tax due on the whole of the chargeable estate and then expressing this as a percentage of the chargeable estate – this gives you an 'effective' IHT rate. The effective rate is then applied to each gift that is to bear its own tax to find out the amount of tax due on the gift. Example 11.3 should make this clear.

EXAMPLE 11.3

Jim dies in July 1994 leaving an estate of £400,000. He makes two specific gifts bearing their own tax: £100,000 to his friend Ben and £80,000 to his friend Gerald. He leaves the residue to his wife. Jim made no PETs or chargeable transfers in the seven years before he died. The tax position is worked out as follows:

Value of free estate	£400,000
less tax-free gifts (£400,000 – £100,000 – £80,000)	£220,000
Chargeable part of estate	£180,000
less tax-free slice	£150,000
	£30,000
Tax on £30,000 @ 40%	£12,000
Effective tax rate ([£12,000 ÷ £180,000] × 100)	6.7%
Tax on Ben's gift @ 6.7%	£6,667
Net amount Ben receives	£93,333
Tax on Gerald's gift @ 6.7%	£5,333
Net amount Gerald receives	£74,667
Amount left to wife	£220,000

If all your specific gifts are free of tax

The main complication in this situation is that, when the estate pays the tax due (out of the residue), it is deemed to be making a gift of the tax as well. To take account of this, all the free-of-tax gifts must be 'grossed up', which simply means that you find the total that equals the amount of the actual gifts plus the tax on them. The tax is then deducted from the residue.

EXAMPLE 11.4

Alec also dies in July 1994 leaving an estate of £400,000. He makes two specific gifts which are free of tax: £100,000 to his friend Douglas and £80,000 to his friend Annette. He leaves the residue to his wife. Alec made no PETs or chargeable transfers in the seven years before he died. The tax position is worked out as follows:

Add together all free-of-tax gifts (£100,000 + £80,000)	£180,000
less tax-free slice	£150,000
	£30,000
divide by 1 – 40% tax rate (i.e. [1 – 0.4] = 0.6)	£50,000
The grossed up value of the gifts is £50,000 + £150,000	£200,000
Value of estate	£400,000
less tax-free part of the estate (£400,000 – £200,000)	£200,000
Chargeable estate	£200,000
less tax-free slice	£150,000
	£50,000
Tax on £50,000 @ 40%	£20,000
Net amount Douglas receives	£100,000

Net amount Annette receives	£80,000
Amount left to wife (£400,000 – £100,000 – £80,000 – £20,000)	£200,000

If you leave a mixture of free-of-tax gifts and other types of taxable gift

This is the most complex situation. The problems arise because the free-of-tax gifts must be grossed by the inheritance tax rate, but initially the appropriate rate is not known because it is worked out in relation to the *whole* chargeable estate (which includes the gifts bearing their own tax as well). The problem is solved by splitting the calculation in two stages.

First, the free-of-tax gifts are grossed up by the full death rate of 40 per cent. The rest of the chargeable estate is added and IHT worked out in the normal way – but the result is only a notional amount of IHT. If notional IHT is divided by the size of the chargeable estate, this gives an assumed rate of IHT.

Now the second stage of the calculation can proceed. The notional rate of IHT is then used to re-gross up the free-of-tax gifts. As before, the rest of the chargeable estate is added and tax is worked out in the normal way (using the 40% death rate). Dividing the tax bill by the total chargeable estate gives the 'final estate rate' which is used to apportion the tax between the different chargeable gifts. See Example 11.5.

You will need to do the same sort of calculation if, in addition to leaving free-of-tax gifts, you also divide the residue so that part is tax-free and part is taxable – this would be the position, for example, if you divided the residue between your children and your husband or wife. The taxable part of the residue is always treated as if it is a gross gift bearing its own tax, so it does not need to be grossed up. See Example 11.6.

EXAMPLE 11.5

Suppose in the example above, Alec left £100,000 free of tax to Douglas and £80,000 free of tax to Annette, as before, but also left a gift of £10,000 to bear its own tax to his daughter Judy. He leaves the residue to his wife. The tax position is as follows:

Stage 1

Add together all free-of-tax gifts (£100,000 + £80,000)	£180,000
less tax-free slice	£150,000
	£30,000
divide by 1 – 40% tax rate (i.e. 1 – 0.4 = 0.6)	£50,000
The grossed up value of the gifts is £50,000 + £150,000	£200,000
Value of estate	£400,000
less exempt part of estate (£400,000 – £200,000 – £10,000)	£190,000
Chargeable estate	£210,000
less tax-free slice	£150,000
	£60,000
Tax on £60,000 @ 40%	£24,000
Assumed rate of IHT ([£24,000 ÷ £210,000] × 100)	11.428%

Stage 2

Total free-of-tax gifts	£180,000
divide by 1 – the notional IHT rate (i.e. 1 – 0.11428 = 0.88572)	
Re-grossed-up value of free-of-tax gift	£203,224
Value of estate	£400,000
less tax-free part of estate (£400,000 – £203,224 – £10,000)	£186,776

New total for chargeable estate	£213,224
less tax-free slice	£150,000
	£63,224
Tax @ 40% on £63,224	£25,289
Final estate rate (£25,289 ÷ £213,224)	11.860%
Tax on Judy's gift @ 11.860%	£1,186
Net amount Judy receives	£8,814
Net amount Douglas receives	£100,000
Net amount Annette receives	£80,000
Tax to be deducted from residue (£25,289 − £1,186)	£24,103
Amount left to wife (£400,000 − £100,000 − £80,000 − £10,000 − £24,103)	£185,897

EXAMPLE 11.6

Percy dies in September 1994 leaving an estate of £400,000. He makes a specific free-of-tax gift of £180,000 to his son, Harold, and leaves the residue equally to his wife and his daughter, Rose. Percy made no PETs or chargeable transfers in the seven years before he died. The tax position is worked out as follows:

Stage 1

Add together all free-of-tax gifts	£180,000
less tax-free slice	£150,000
	£30,000
divide by 1 − 40% tax rate (i.e. [1 − 0.4] = 0.6)	£50,000

The grossed up value of the gift is £50,000 + £150,000	£200,000
Value of estate	£400,000
less tax-free part of the estate (£400,000 − £200,000 − [1/2 × residue])	£100,000
Chargeable estate	£300,000
less tax-free slice	£150,000
	£150,000
Tax on £150,000 @ 40%	£60,000
Assumed rate of IHT ([£60,000 ÷ £300,000] × 100)	20.000%

Stage 2

Free-of-tax gift	£180,000
divide by 1− the notional IHT rate (i.e. 1 − 0.2 = 0.8)	
Re-grossed-up value of free-of-tax gift	£225,000
Value of estate	£400,000
less tax-free part of estate (£400,000 − £225,000 − [1/2 × residue])	£87,500
New total for chargeable estate	£312,500
less tax-free slice	£150,000
	£162,500
Tax @ 40% on £162,500	£65,000
Final estate rate (£65,000 ÷ £312,500)	20.800%

Harold receives	£180,000
Tax on Harold's legacy @ 20.800% of £225,000 (to be borne by estate)	£46,800
Residue (£400,000 – £180,000 – £46,800)	£173,200
Wife receives (1/2 × £173,200)	£86,600
Tax on Rose's share of the residue @ 20.80% × £86,600	£18,012
Rose receives (£86,600 – £18,012)	£68,588

Quick succession relief

If you left a substantial gift to someone in your will – for example, a son or daughter – who then died shortly after you, there could be two IHT bills on the same assets in a short space of time. To guard against this, a claim can be made for 'quick succession relief'. This is available where the person inheriting the assets dies within five years of them becoming part of that person's estate (even if they are then sold or given away before the recipient's death). The relief is tapered: full relief is given if the recipient's death occurs within one year of the gift; reduced rate applies if a longer time elapses (see Table 11.1).

Table 11.1 Quick succession relief

Years between first and second death	Tax relief on second death as a percentage of tax applicable to the original gift[37]
Up to 1	100
More than 1 and up to 2	80
More than 2 and up to 3	60
More than 3 and up to 4	40
More than 4 and up to 5	20
More than 5	no tax relief

[37]The percentage is multiplied by the formula:

$$\frac{G-T}{G} \times T$$

where G = the gross amount of the original gift
T = the tax paid on the original gift.

Quick succession relief is also available where the original gift was a lifetime gift and the recipient dies within five years. However, the amount of tax due, if any, on the original gift will not be known until seven years have passed since the gift was made, so there will be a delay before the amount of any relief can be calculated.

Passing on your business

Handing on your business is a complex matter. There are many different ways of arranging the transfer and which is appropriate for you will depend very much on your particular circumstances. You would be unwise to make plans without seeking professional advice from your accountant and a solicitor. Business planning is outside the scope of this book, but it is worth pointing out here the important reliefs against IHT that may be available to you and your heirs.

Business property relief

If, on death, you hand on your business to someone else, your personal representatives may be able to claim 'business property relief' which will reduce the value of the transfer of the business for IHT purposes and thus reduce or eliminate any IHT otherwise payable. To be eligible, you must have been in business for at least two years. Only 'qualifying' business assets attract relief; these are assets which are either:

● used wholly or mainly for the purpose of your business, *or*
● are required for future use by the business.

Assuming you operate your business as a sole trader or as a partner in a partnership, business property relief will be given at the higher rate of 100 per cent (from 9 March 1992) — that is, it could completely eliminate an IHT charge.

EXAMPLE 11.7

Gerald dies leaving a grocery business valued at £500,000 which he has run for the last ten years. In his will, he hands the business to his son. Paul. He also leaves £250,000 to his wife. The IHT position is as follows:

Value of free estate	£750,000
less tax-free gift to wife	£250,000
Value of grocery business	£500,000
less 100% business property relief	£500,000
Chargeable part of the estate	£0

Relief of 100 per cent is also available if you pass on a holding of shares of more than 25 per cent of the shares of an unquoted company or a company quoted on the Unlisted Securities Market (USM).

A lower rate of business property relief – set at 50 per cent since 9 March 1992 – is available to set against transfers of a *controlling* holding in a fully quoted company or a holding or less than 25 per cent in an unquoted or USM company.

The rates of relief were increased in the 1992 budget and are intended to take most handovers of family companies outside the IHT net. However, even 100 per cent relief will not necessarily entirely mitigate an IHT bill. In particular, you should note that if the business property is subject to a binding contract for sale, relief will not be given. This might be the case where, say, a partnership has arranged that the surviving partners will buy out the share of a partner who dies; the deceased partner's share of the business would not qualify for relief in this situation.

Most types of business can qualify for business property relief. The only exception is businesses whose sole or main activity is dealing in stocks, shares, land or various other investments.

Any IHT due after business property relief has been given can be paid by interest-free instalments over a period of ten years.

Agricultural property relief

'Agricultural property relief' – which is similar to business property relief – is available when a farm is handed on. The relief, which is given automatically and does not have to be claimed, is given against the agricultural value of the land and buildings. The equipment, stock and so on do not qualify for agricultural property relief, but they may qualify for business property relief (see above). Note that the agricultural value of the farm may be lower than the market value if, say, the land has development value – the excess will not qualify for agricultural property relief, though it may be eligible for business property relief.

To qualify for agricultural property relief, you must either have occupied the farm, or a share of it, for the purpose of farming for at least two years, or you must have owned the farm, or a share in it, for at least seven years. If you farmed the land yourself, relief is given at the higher rate of 100 per cent from 9 March onwards. If you let the land to someone else to farm, relief is restricted to the lower rate of 50 per cent.

As with business property relief, agricultural property relief is also not available if the farm is subject to a binding contract for sale (see above).

Any IHT due after relief has been given can be paid by interest-free instalments over a period of ten years.

Paying the tax

Your personal representative(s) are responsible for paying the IHT due on your estate (and any other taxes which are outstanding at your death). IHT is due six months after the end of the month in which death occurs. However, if your personal representatives finish preparing the accounts of your estate earlier than this, the IHT becomes payable immediately the accounts are submitted. Your representatives may be able to pay the IHT in ten equal yearly instalments.

CHAPTER 12

INHERITANCE PLANNING

IT'S NEVER TOO LATE, BUT . . .

'So you mean that we can, in effect, rewrite Dad's will to swap the gifts around and cut the tax bill?'

'Precisely, Miss Cale. The law does currently allow this,' said the solicitor, somewhat ponderously. 'However, I should point out that matters would have been a great deal simpler had Mr Cale made satisfactory arrangements *before* his death. There would have been considerably greater scope for minimising – or even eliminating – the inheritance tax bill had he done so.'

This chapter draws together a number of points discussed in earlier chapters and introduces some new ones to show what you can do to plan your giving through inheritance more precisely and tax-efficiently.

The particular strategies you adopt will depend largely on your personal intentions and circumstances. Although many of the points given below can be applied simply and with a minimum of paperwork, others are not so straightforward and may hide potential pitfalls that you should take into account. Always seek advice from, for example, a solicitor or accountant if you are in any doubt about a proposed course of action. And, if you are giving away large sums, get advice first.

There are two main aims to planning inheritance:

1. To make sure that your estate is divided as you had wished.
2. To minimise the amount of tax to be paid on the estate.

Clearly, the two aims are interlinked since a lower inheritance tax (IHT) bill means that there is more of your estate left to give to your family and friends. Strategies to meet either or both aims are discussed below.

Gifts when you die

Use your tax-free slice

Try to make use of your tax-free slice (which covers the first £150,000 of chargeable transfers in the 1994–95 tax year), and bear in mind that some gifts – for example, to your husband or wife or to charity – are always tax-free.

It may be tempting simply to leave everything to your husband or wife, but this can mean an unnecessarily large tax bill when they die (see Example 12.1). If you and your husband or wife intend to leave something to your children, it may be best to draw up your wills so that whoever dies first leaves part of the estate directly to the children. This will ensure that at least some use is made of the available tax-free slice. The remainder of the estate can be left to the surviving spouse. If you can, arrange the wills so that both of you can make maximum use of your tax-free slices, but take care to ensure that the surviving spouse will have enough to meet financial needs.

EXAMPLE 12.1

Sam dies and leaves his whole estate of £100,000 to his wife, Harriet. Since this is a tax-free gift, there is no IHT to pay. When Harriet dies her free estate is valued at £200,000 and is left completely to their only child, Phyllis. There is IHT to pay on the estate calculated as follows:

Value of free estate	£200,000
less tax-free slice	£150,000
	£50,000

Tax on £50,000 @ 40%   £20,000

However, suppose instead that Sam had left £50,000 to Phyllis (on which no IHT would be payable because it would be covered by the tax-free slice) and the remaining £50,000 to Harriet. On Harriet's death, her estate would have been valued at £150,000. Giving this to Phyllis would have been completely covered by Harriet's tax-free slice, so no IHT would be payable. Straightforward planning to make use of Sam's tax-free slice would save £20,000 in tax.

Be aware of how gifts are taxed

Examples 11.3 and 11.4 in Chapter 11 are intentionally identical except that in one the gifts bear their own tax and in the other the gifts are free of tax. The outcomes highlight two important points which you should bear in mind when planning gifts under your will:

1. A gift which bears its own tax will generally be smaller than a gift of the same size which is free of tax.
2. Leaving free-of-tax gifts reduces the size of the residue. If you leave a lot of free-of-tax gifts, the residue may be reduced to a trivial amount (or nothing at all).

Using lifetime gifts

One way to reduce the IHT payable on your death is to reduce the size of your estate by making gifts during your lifetime. However, before going down this course, you must consider your own financial needs. Any IHT payable on your estate is not really your problem; it will simply reduce the amount by which others benefit from your estate. It is not worth jeopardising your financial security in order to reduce the IHT bill of your heirs. So the first planning point is: do not give away more than you can afford to do without.

Assuming that you can afford to make a number of gifts during your lifetime, you will obviously want to ensure that they do not themselves give rise to a large tax bill. Chapter 5 lists the gifts which you can make during your lifetime which are tax-free.

It is not enough to look only at the IHT position of lifetime gifts. You must also consider the Capital Gains Tax (CGT) position (see Chapters 5 and 6). Taking the two taxes together, the 'best' gifts to make will tend to be the following:

- Cash gifts (always free of CGT) that qualify for an IHT exemption.
- Cash gifts that count as PETs (see p. 79) for IHT purposes.
- Business assets that qualify for hold-over relief from CGT (see p. 70) and count as PETs for IHT.
- Other gifts that are exempt from IHT or that count as PETs and for which the CGT bill is relatively small due to unused CGT allowance or indexation allowance (see Chapter 6).

Make tax-free gifts

Particularly important for IHT purposes is your yearly tax-free exemption (see p. 55), which lets you give away up to £3,000 each year without incurring any IHT liability. If you choose cash gifts, there will be no CGT either.

Another very useful gift which is free of IHT is normal expenditure out of income – this can be particularly handy when used in conjunction with an insurance policy (see pp. 54 and 148).

It is not generally worth making, in your lifetime, a gift which would in any case be tax-free on your death: for example, a gift to charity. A safer course would be to retain the assets in case you need to draw on them and make the desired gift in your will.

Give assets whose value will rise

If your aim is to reduce the value of your estate at the time you die, then it makes sense to give away assets whose value you expect to increase. In that way the increase will accrue to the recipient of the gift and will be outside your estate.

Gifts with reservation

It is very difficult to take advantage of the tax rules and at the same time retain the use or control of something you are giving away outright. If the recipient does not enjoy the full use of the gift and you will in some way benefit, the gift may be deemed a 'gift with reservation' under the IHT rules and it will still count as part of your estate until the reservation ends. For more details see pp. 81–83.

Making use of trusts

One way in which you can retain control over something you give away is by putting it into trust (see Chapter 9).

Lifetime gifts to a trust

Generally, you cannot be a beneficiary or potential beneficiary of a trust you set up without the assets you put into it counting as a gift with reservation. However, your husband or wife can benefit under the trust without triggering these rules *provided* that you yourself in no way benefit from your spouse's interest in the trust. Even in the latter case, however, the income tax and CGT rules may make this type of arrangement unattractive (see p. 107).

A further exception to the gift with reservation rules is that if you retain a reversionary interest (see p. 97) in a trust to which you have given assets, the gift does not count as one with reservation.

If you have made a gift with reservation to a discretionary trust (see p. 98) and the reservation ends (for example, you cease to be a potential beneficiary), you are deemed to have made a PET to the trust on the date the reservation ends. Since normally a gift to a discretionary trust counts as a chargeable gift, you can possibly use this anomaly to your advantage (see Example 12.2).

Beware of setting up more than one trust on the same day, if one of them is a discretionary trust. If you do, it may increase the periodic charge on the discretionary trust.

If you yourself inherit money or assets which are surplus to your needs, you might consider putting them into trust straightaway to benefit your children or grandchildren – this is a practice known as 'generation skipping'. The transfer can often be made tax-efficiently through a 'deed of variation' or possibly a 'disclaimer' (see below).

EXAMPLE 12.2

In September 1993, Jarvis wanted to put £100,000 into a discretionary trust for the benefit of his adult children. But his running total of gifts over the last seven years already exceeded £150,000. If he had made the gift then, he would have incurred an immediate tax bill of 20% × £100,000 = £20,000. Instead, he made himself a potential beneficiary under the trust; the £100,000 counted as a gift with reservation, and thus it did not reduce the value of his estate and there was no immediate tax bill. In 1996, Jarvis alters the trust so that he can no longer benefit under it. This action 'triggers' his gift which now ceases to be part of his estate and counts as a PET. Provided Jarvis survives for seven years after 1996, there will be no IHT on the gift.

Wills and trusts

There are two situations in which setting up a trust in your will can be particularly useful. The first is where you want to give some of your assets to the next generation but your wife or husband will carry on needing the income from, or use of, those assets. One way around this is to leave the assets in trust, giving your spouse an interest in possession (see p. 97) during his or her lifetime, with your children (or perhaps their children) holding the reversionary interest (see p. 97). But note that, while this ensures that your assets are used largely as you would wish, it does not have any IHT advantage. This is because, under IHT, a person with an interest in possession is deemed to own the underlying trust assets and to give them away when the interest ends. So there could be a large IHT bill at the time of the second death. You could avoid this problem by using a discretionary trust instead, with both your spouse and your children named as beneficiaries. This would be tax-efficient provided the transfer of assets into the trust was covered by your tax-free slice.

However, an interest in possession trust can be useful for IHT planning if assets are being passed to subsequent generations. This is because a reversionary interest does not count as part of a person's estate and so there is no IHT liability if it is transferred to someone else. If your children held the reversionary interest in a trust, they could easily transfer this interest to their own children if they wished to do so, without incurring any IHT liability.

The second important planning use of will trusts is where you are passing on your business. Rather than pass total control to, for example, a relatively inexperienced son or daughter, or to a spouse who is not involved in the business, it may make sense to put the land or property used by the business into trust. Provided the occupier qualifies for business property relief or agricultural property relief, the trust will also qualify (see pp. 137–139). This is a complex area and you should seek the advice of your accountant and/or solicitor.

Note that a trust set up under your will is deemed to start on the date of death, so do not fall into the trap of setting up several trusts including one or more discretionary trusts under your will. A way round this would be to set up the discretionary trust(s) before death, putting in just a token amount to get them started and then adding more in your will.

Making loans

One way to 'freeze' the value of part of your estate is to make an interest-free loan to someone and leaving them to keep the proceeds from investing the loan. A condition of the loan would normally be that it is repayable on demand. From your point of view, this is more secure than making an outright gift and can be a useful arrangement if you are unsure whether or not you will need the money back at some time in the future.

Of course, there is little point demanding repayment of a loan if the borrower simply does not have the money available to repay you. An even more secure route would be to make the loan to a discretionary trust and to name the intended recipient as a potential beneficiary under the trust.

'Associated operations'

Beware! Different transactions (gifts, loans, lease, and so on) that affect the same assets can be deemed to be linked together – in which case, they are called 'associated operations'. This could result in a complicated 'gift' being disallowed for tax purposes if the Inland Revenue decides that a series of transactions are designed mainly as a way of evading a tax bill. The legislation lists the following examples where transactions will not be treated as linked:

- If you arrange a lease, for example, giving you the right to live in a house, and you pay the full market rate for that lease, this will not be linked with any other transaction that takes place more than three years after the lease was made.
- No transaction made on or after 27 March 1974 can be linked to a transaction made before that date.

You should also be aware that where a gift is made as a result of a series of associated operations over a period of time, for IHT purposes, the transfer will be considered to have taken place on the date of the last of the linked transactions – you will get relief against any tax paid at the earlier stages. This is an important point in relation to the size of your running total of gifts.

Using life insurance

There are three main ways in which life insurance can be a useful inheritance planning tool, and these are discussed in turn below. All rely on making use of two factors, as follows:

1. *Tax-free gifts* Taking out insurance for the benefit of someone else means that the premiums count as gifts. You can ensure that there is no possibility of IHT on these premiums if you make sure they count as tax-free gifts. The most commonly used exemptions are to make the premiums out of your normal income or to ensure that they fall within your yearly tax-free exemption of £3,000.
2. *Trust status* If the proceeds of an insurance policy are payable to you, the pay-out will be added to your estate when you die, which will increase the size of your estate and will cause delay before your beneficiaries have access to the pay-out. Therefore, it is important that the policy proceeds are paid direct to the intended beneficiary. You make sure this happens by 'writing' the insurance policy 'in trust', which means that the policy is held in trust for the benefit of whoever you name and the proceeds are the property of that person rather than of you or your estate. Insurance companies will generally write a policy in trust for you

at no extra charge (since they are able, in most cases, to use standard documents).

The cost of insurance increases with the likelihood of the insurance company having to pay out. So if you are in poor health, or you are very old, buying life insurance may be prohibitively expensive.

PETs and insurance

If you make a gift which counts as a PET, you may want to be absolutely sure that any IHT bill which subsequently arises could be paid. (Similarly, you might want to ensure that any extra tax on a chargeable gift arising on death could be paid.) One way of ensuring this would be to take out a 'term insurance' policy. Term insurance pays out if you die within a specified time – in this case, seven years; should you survive the specified period, it pays out nothing. Since the liability for IHT on a PET decreases as the years go by, the cover you need can also reduce – in other words, you want 'decreasing term insurance'. See Example 12.3.

EXAMPLE 12.3

Jeremy gives his niece, Penny, a gift of £10,000. It counts as a PET and so there is no tax to pay at the time of the gift. However, Jeremy's running total exceeds £150,000, and if he were to die within seven years of making the gift, Penny would face a demand for tax on the gift. The potential tax liability would be as follows:

Years between gift and death	% rate of tax on the gift (at 1992–93 tax rates)	Potential tax bill (£s)
Up to 3	40	4,000
More than 3 and up to 4	32	3,200
More than 4 and up to 5	24	2,400
More than 5 and up to 6	16	1,600
More than 6 and up to 7	8	800
More than 7	no tax	0

Jeremy takes out a seven-year term insurance which would pay Penny £4,000 if he died within the first three years and a reducing sum thereafter to cover the tax bill which would arise.

Reducing the size of your estate

You could use life insurance to build up a gift which does not count as part of your estate. For example, you might use the full £3,000 yearly tax-free exemption to pay the premiums on a policy that will pay out to the recipient either after some specified period (in which case, you need an 'endowment policy' – see p. 160) or when you die (in which case, you need a 'whole life policy' – see p. 165).

In choosing this strategy, you will need to weigh it against alternative strategies: for example, setting up a trust which could invest in a wide range of investments. The 'up-front' costs of setting up your own trust will be higher, but the ongoing costs could work out to be less than for a life insurance policy. If you have relatively small sums to give, the insurance route would be more appropriate.

Paying IHT when you die

You could take out a whole life policy (which pays out *whenever* you die) to provide a lump sum to meet an expected IHT bill on your estate. In essence, this is no different from using insurance as a way of making a gift on death as already discussed, but the factors to consider are slightly different: you could save in your own investment fund (either within your estate or within a trust) to meet a potential IHT bill, but it would take time to build up the full amount needed. If you died in the meantime, your investment would be insufficient to cover the IHT. Taking out a whole life insurance policy removes that risk because (provided you have bought the appropriate level of cover) it would pay out the full amount needed whether you die sooner or later.

Gifts from the deathbed

If, say, you are seriously ill and do not expect to live for long, you might make a gift in contemplation of your death – known as a *donatio mortis causa*. Such a gift does not take affect until your death and it lapses completely if you do not die after all (or if the recipient dies before you).

In a situation as described above, should your intention be to make an outright gift to someone that is not conditional on your dying, it would be wise to set down your intention in writing – in, say, a signed letter to the recipient – to safeguard against the gift being mistakenly treated as a *donatio mortis causa* (and thus being treated as part of your estate if you survive).

A further point to watch out for, in a deathbed situation, is that a gift which is made by cheque is not made until the cheque has been *cleared* against the giver's account. If death takes place before then, the gift would become invalid.

Altering a will after death

Oddly enough, your will is not the final word in regard to your estate. Following death, there is a two-year period during which the will can be varied – in effect, rewritten – and your gifts reallocated. The allocation of the estate can also be varied where a person dies intestate (see Chapter 10).

The variation must be agreed by all the beneficiaries named under the will and is made by one or more of them who must complete a written deed. No beneficiary may receive any payment either in cash or kind in return for benefits given up due to the variation.

A variation can affect part, or the whole, of an estate, except that the amount an infant child would receive cannot be reduced without the consent of the court and the way in which assets put into trust is left may not be varied.

Where – as is usual – the redistribuition affects the potential IHT due on the estate, an election must be made within six months of the deed of variation to the Inland Revenue for tax to be reassessed. In addition, if the variation would alter the CGT liability, an election can also be made to the Inland Revenue to reassess this. (Although there is no CGT on death, the personal representatives might have to sell assets after death, which could give rise to a CGT bill. And, if assets originally left to one beneficiary are to be passed instead to another, there could, in the absence of an election, be a CGT bill.)

There are, in fact, two ways in which the passing on of an estate can be varied: by deed of variation or by 'disclaimer'. The main difference between the two methods is that, under a deed of variation, who is to receive various assets can be changed from one person to another. Under a disclaimer, the named beneficiary in the will merely says they will not have the gift, in which case the assets are reallocated according to the terms of the will (for example, they might simply be added to the residue) or to the rules of intestacy. It follows from this that a disclaimer can only increase the share of the estate going to some or all of the other beneficiaries. By contrast, a deed of variation can be used to make gifts to people who did not originally stand to benefit from the will or intestacy.

Note that a disclaimer cannot be made if the original beneficiary has already received some benefit from the inherited assets that they intend to disclaim.

In considering whether or not to vary the way an estate is left, and the form that any variation should take, all the normal planning considerations come into play: for example, making sure the tax-free slice is used, choosing whether gifts should be free of tax or bear their own tax, creating or renouncing life interests and so on. See Example 12.4.

In the 1989 budget, the government announced its intention to restrict severely the possibilities for using deeds of variation (but not disclaimers). In the event, the proposal was dropped from the subsequent Finance Bill after concerns that, without the ability to vary wills, unwelcome pressure would tend to be brought to bear on people, when they were already under stress due to illness or old age, to sort out their affairs efficiently. Nevertheless, the government said it would keep the matter under review, and there may be further attempts to reduce the use of deeds of variation. The message is clear: plan ahead so that variation is unnecessary.

EXAMPLE 12.4

When Fred died, his will revealed that he had left £500,000 to his wife, Betty, and the residue of his estate to his daughter, Linda. His daughter's share was £50,000 on which no tax was due, because Fred's taxable estate plus a couple of PETs made in the last seven years came to a running total of only £60,000.

Betty intends, when she dies, to leave everything to Linda, but this will mean a large IHT bill on an estate made up of Betty's own £20,000 or so and the £500,000 left to her by Fred. Assuming she had made no chargeable gifts in the seven years before death, tax of [£520,000 – £150,000 = £370,000] × 0.4 = £148,000 would be payable. But this bill could be reduced if some changes are made to Fred's will.

Betty does not need the whole £500,000, so she and Linda make a deed of variation directing that Fred's estate be split as follows: £140,000 to Linda – which, with the earlier PETs, uses up the whole of Fred's tax-free slice – and the residue of £410,000 to his wife. There is still no IHT to pay on Fred's estate, and the potential bill when Betty dies is reduced to [£410,000 + £20,000 – £150,000 = £280,000] × 0.4 = £112,000. This is a saving of £36,000.

RATES OF INHERITANCE TAX 1986–95

The first slice of taxable gifts which are tax-free is increased each tax year – generally in line with inflation up to the preceding December. Rates may also be changed once a year, though since 1989 rates have been unchanged. Changes are often effective from the date of the budget in which they are announced rather than 6 April. Rates shown are those applicable at death.

1986–87

Tax-free slice	£71,000

Thereafter, for gross taxable gifts:

Tax rate on next £24,000	30%
Tax rate on next £34,000	35%
Tax rate on next £35,000	40%
Tax rate on next £42,000	45%
Tax rate on next £51,000	50%
Tax rate on next £60,000	55%
Tax rate above this	60%

1987–88

Tax-free slice	£90,000

Thereafter, for gross taxable gifts:

Tax rate on next £50,000	30%
Tax rate on next £80,000	40%
Tax rate on next £110,000	50%
Tax rate above this	60%

1988–89

Tax-free slice	£110,000
Thereafter for gross taxable gifts:	
Tax rate	40%

1989–90

Tax-free slice	£118,000
Thereafter for gross taxable gifts:	
Tax rate	40%

1990–91

Tax-free slice	£128,000
Thereafter for gross taxable gifts:	
Tax rate	40%

1991–92

Tax-free slice	£140,000
Thereafter for gross taxable gifts:	
Tax rate	40%

1992–93

Tax-free slice	£150,000
Thereafter for gross taxable gifts:	
Tax rate	40%

1993–94

Tax-free slice	£150,000
Thereafter for gross taxable gifts:	
Tax rate	40%

1994–95

Tax-free slice	£150,000
Thereafter for gross taxable gifts:	
Tax rate	40%

Glossary

Accumulation and maintenance trust A type of *discretionary trust* which enjoys special tax treatment: gifts to the trust count as *potentially exempt transfers*; there is no *inheritance tax* on the property within the trust nor when property is paid out to *beneficiaries*. The special treatment is only granted provided certain rules are kept: for example, at least one beneficiary must become entitled to part or all of the trust property by the age of 25. These trusts are especially useful as a way of giving to one or more young children, for example, grandchildren.

Administrator The *personal representative* who settles the affairs of someone who has died without leaving a will. They are appointed by the court and will often be the husband or wife of the deceased person.

Affinity card A credit card which, when used, generates donations to charity. The card issuing company usually agrees to make a donation when you first take out a card and then further donations of, for example, £6 for every £100 turnover on the card. In other respects, the card is like a normal credit card.

Allowable business expense Spending you make in the course of running your business that can be set against the income of the business when working out the profits for income tax purposes. Generally, to count as allowable, the spending must have been made 'wholly and exclusively' for the purpose of the business.

Asset Anything which you own: for example, your home, car, personal possessions, money, investments, and so on.

Beneficiary A person who may receive property from a trust, or who has been left something in a will.

Bequest   A gift to someone in a will. Also called a *legacy*.

BES   Abbreviation for *Business Expansion Scheme*.

British Government stocks   A type of investment issued by the government which generally pays a regular income and a capital sum after a specified period of time. (A few stocks do not offer the capital sum, only income.) When you buy a British Government stock, you are, in effect, making a loan to the government. These are considered to be very secure investments because of the very low risk that the government would be unable to repay you. Also known as *gilts*.

Business Expansion Scheme   An investment in the shares of either a new company or a company starting a new venture. The government encourages this type of investment by giving relief from *income tax* at your top rate on the money you invest provided you invest for at least five years. Capital gains on BES investments made after 18 March 1986 are free of *capital gains tax*. The returns can be very high, but there is also a high risk of loss because of a significant proportion of BES companies fail.

CAF   Abbreviation for the *Charities Aid Foundation*.

Capital gains tax (CGT)   Tax on gains that you make from selling an *asset* for more than it was worth when you first started to own it. If you give the asset away, you are deemed to have made a gain if the asset has risen in value over the time you have owned it. In practice, there is often no tax to pay on a gain because you are allowed to make various deductions in calculating the gain for tax purposes. The most important deductions are *indexation allowance* and the 'tax-free slice'. The tax-free slice enables you to make a given amount of otherwise taxable gains (£5,800 in the 1992–93 tax year) free of CGT. The rate at which tax is levied on taxable gains is 20 per cent, 25 per cent or 40 per cent.

CGT   Abbreviation for *capital gains tax*.

Chargeable transfer   A gift that is not a *potentially exempt transfer* and that is not tax-free for another reason (for example, if it were a gift between husband and wife), and on which there may be an *inheritance tax bill*.

Charitable trust   A type of *trust* whose aims and purposes meet the requirements for charitable status. This means that there is no *income tax*, *capital gains tax* or *inheritance tax* on the trust property or payments from it provided they are used for charitable ends. In addition, income tax relief is given on gifts to the trust provided they are made through one of the special schemes available – such as through a *covenant* or *gift aid*.

Charities Aid Foundation A charity whose aim is to promote and assist other charities. It is a rich source of information about charities and operates a Charity Account which provides individuals (and companies) with a tax-efficient and flexible method of giving to charity.

Charity Commission The government department responsible for registering charities, investigating abuse of charitable status and helping charities to run efficiently and within the charity laws.

Chattels A tax term for those of your possessions which are physical and portable things: for example, jewellery, furniture, cars. Technically they are referred to as 'tangible movable property'.

Children This may be defined in various ways for the purpose of specific pieces of legislation. For example, under the *intestacy* rules, 'children' means children of your current marriage, children of any former marriage(s), illegitimate children and adopted children, but it does not include stepchildren. Under the *income tax* rules, 'children' is more widely defined and does include stepchildren.

Codicil An amendment to a *will* to be considered in conjunction with the will. If the amendments are many or complicated, it will usually be better to rewrite the will rather than use a codicil.

Covenant A legally binding agreement to make regular payments of income to a person or organisation. Before 15 March 1988, gifts to people and charities under a covenant could attract relief from *income tax*, but, from that date onwards, tax relief is restricted to covenanted gifts to charities. The precise wording of the covenant is important otherwise the covenant could fail to qualify for the tax relief.

Deed of variation See *variation*.

Demonstrative legacy A gift of money or things made under a will and to be provided out of a specified part of the deceased person's *estate*.

Deposited deed Another name for a *loan covenant*.

Deposited covenant Another name for a *loan covenant*.

Disabled trust A type of *discretionary trust*, qualifying for special tax treatment, for the maintenance or other benefit of a mentally disabled person (as defined under the Mental Health Act 1983). Gifts to the trust by the disabled person are free of *inheritance tax* and gifts by other people to the trust count as *potentially exempt transfers (PETs)*; property held within the trust is free of *inheritance tax*, as are payments to the disabled person; the disabled person is treated as owning the trust property and thus if he/she gives it away the gift counts as a PET.

Disclaimer   The voluntary giving up of a gift made to you under a will following the death of the giver. The gift is then distributed according to the other terms of the will (for example, it might increase the value of the *residue*).

Discretionary trust   A *trust* in which none of the beneficiaries has an *interest in possession* and the distribution of trust property or income from it is at the discretion of the *trustees*. The tax treatment of this type of trust is not as favourable as the regime for other trusts: gifts to a discretionary trust count as *chargeable transfers*; the trust fund is subject to *income tax*, *capital gains tax* and *inheritance tax (IHT)* with IHT being levied every ten years according to a complex formula; there is also IHT to pay on payments from the trust to the beneficiaries.

Endowment policy   A type of life insurance policy which builds up an investment value over a specified term (the 'endowment' period). At the end of the term, the policy matures and the investment can be cashed in. Earlier encashment is possible, but returns may be low.

Enterprise Investment Scheme   Announced in the November 1993 Budget, this is a replacement for the *Business Expansion Scheme* and is a tax-efficient scheme for investment in the shares of a new unquoted company or company starting a new venture. Tax relief at 20 per cent will be given on investment up to £100,000 a year and gains will be free of capital gains tax provided certain conditions are met.

Estate   All a person's possessions – home, car, money, investments, and so on – less their debts.

Executor   The *personal representative* who sorts out the affairs of someone who has died in accordance with their *will* (and any subsequent *variation* to it). The executor will normally be a person (or company) appointed by the deceased person in his/her will.

Family provision claim   A claim by someone who, in the first instance, does not benefit from your *estate*, either under the terms of your *will* or under the *intestacy* rules, for financial support from the estate. The claimant will need to show that he/she was dependent on you during your lifetime.

Fixed interest trust   Another name for an *interest in possession trust*.

Friendly society plans   A type of investment, basically the same as some investment-type *life insurance* but which qualifies for special tax treatment. You pay premiums to the society that are invested for a given time, after which you receive a pay out. There is no *income tax* or *capital gains tax* on the investment fund and there is no tax on the pay-out. The sum you can invest in these plans is restricted to a relatively low amount.

Gift with reservation   This occurs when you give away something but retain the right to use or enjoy the thing: for example, you might give away your home but continue to live there, or give away a piece of furniture but continue to keep it in your home. For *inheritance tax* purposes, a gift with reservation does not count as a gift at the time it is made but continues to be part of your estate. Tax becomes due (if payable) at the time the reservation stops: for example, on death. It is possible to make an outright gift and for the reservation to arise some time after the gift is made (for example, if you move back into a home you gave away).

Gift aid   A special scheme for use in making lump sum gifts to charity of £250 or more. The gift qualifies for tax relief at your top rate of *income tax*.

'Gilts'   Another name for *British Government stocks*.

Gross   Used in the context of tax computations to mean 'before tax'.

'Grossing up'   The process of finding out the before-tax amount of a payment from the *net* amount. The 'grossed up' value is the sum of the net value plus the amount of tax which has been paid (or deemed to have been paid). Grossing up is carried out by dividing the net sum by [1 − (tax rate ÷ 100)]. For example, take net income of £75 which has been taxed at the basic rate of *income tax* of 25 per cent. The grossed-up value is: £75 ÷ [1 − (25 ÷ 100)] = £75 ÷ [1 − 0.25] = £75 ÷ 0.75 = £100. In other words, tax of £25 has been paid and the grossed-up value is the sum of £75 + £25.

Hold-over relief   The process of deferring a *capital gains tax* due at the time a gift is made by passing the liability to the recipient of the gift. This is done by deducting from the recipient's *initial value* of the gift the amount of tax otherwise payable.

IHT   Abbreviation for *inheritance tax*.

Income tax   Tax payable on most types of income: for example, earnings from a job, interest on investments, and so on. Everyone has a personal allowance (£3,445 in the 1994–95 tax year) which means that income of up to that amount is tax-free. Other allowances and deductions may also apply. Tax is charged at a rate of 20 per cent on the first £3,000 of taxable income. Thereafter, it is charged at a basic rate of 25 per cent on the taxable income up to £23,700 of chargeable income, and at 40 per cent on income above that amount, in the 1994–95 tax year.

Independent taxation   New system of taxing married couples introduced from 6 April 1990 under which husband and wife are treated as separate units for *income tax* and *capital gains tax* purposes. This means, for example, that they each have their own personal allowance and basic rate tax band. (Under the earlier system, income and gains of the wife were generally treated for tax as being those of the husband.)

Indexation allowance   That part of a capital gain on an asset that is judged to be due to the asset's value keeping pace with inflation (either since you first owned it or since March 1982, whichever date is later). This part of the gain is not liable for *capital gains tax (CGT)* and is deducted from the capital gain in calculating any CGT liability.

Inheritance tax (IHT)   Tax due on a *chargeable transfer* either in your lifetime or when your *estate* is passed on at the time of death. Tax is worked out by looking at the running total of all such transfers over the last seven years. If this total comes to more than the tax-free slice (of £150,000 in the 1994–95 tax year), tax will be payable. IHT is charged at a rate of 20 per cent on chargeable transfers made during your life (though extra tax may be due if you die within seven years) and at a rate of 40 per cent on transfers at the time of death.

Interest in possession   The right to receive income from trust property. You may also have the right to receive the capital at some specified time or this may pass then to someone else.

Interest in possession trust   A type of *trust* where one or more beneficiaries have the right to receive the income from the trust property at the time the income arises (called an *interest in possession*). The same person or someone else may have the right to the trust property when the trust comes to an end (called the *reversionary interest*). The tax treatment of this type of trust is fairly favourable: gifts paid into the trust count as *potentially exempt transfers (PETs)*; there is no *inheritance tax* on the trust property or on the income payments from it; the person holding the interest in possession is treated as owning the trust property, so when the trust comes to an end, that person is deemed to make a PET.

Intestacy   Dying without having made a will. Your estate is distributed according to the rules of intestacy. These rules aim to protect your husband or wife up to a certain degree and your children. But the application of the rules can cause problems with, for example, part of your estate going to relatives outside the immediate family, or an unmarried partner being left nothing (though they would be eligible to make a *family provision claim*).

Investment trust   A type of investment where you buy shares in a company whose business is investing in other companies and/or other assets.

Joint tenancy   A way of sharing the ownership of an asset. You and the other joint tenant(s) have equal shares in the property and the same rights to enjoy the use of the *whole* asset. You cannot sell or give away your share of the asset independently of the other joint tenant(s) and on death your share automatically passes to them.

Life interest   The right to receive the income from an asset for as long as you live but not the asset itself. On your death, the asset passes to whoever has the *reversionary interest*.

Loan covenant   A combination of a *covenant* and a loan that enables a gift to charity to benefit from the tax advantages of a covenant, but you give a single lump sum rather than committing yourself to regular payments over a number of years.

National Savings investments   A group of 'deposit-type' investments that are issued by the government. You invest and either receive a tax-free return or receive an income paid before the deduction of income tax. They include: National Savings Investment Account, National Savings Certificate, the Children's Bonus Bond and National Savings Income Bonds.

Net   Used in the context of tax computations to mean 'after tax has been deducted'.

Net assets   Your *assets* less your debts and outstanding expenses.

Payroll Deduction   Another name for *Payroll Giving*.

Payroll Giving   A special scheme for making gifts to charity directly out of your earnings from a job. The gifts qualify for relief from *income tax* at your top rate.

Pecuniary legacy   A gift in a will of a specified sum of money.

PEP   Abbreviation for *Personal Equity Plan*.

Personal Equity Plan (PEP)   An investment in shares, unit trust, or investment trusts where the income and gains are free of *income tax* and *capital gains tax*, respectively, as long as the investments remain in the PEP.

Personal representative   The person (or company) who sorts out the *estate* of someone who has died. There are two types of representative: the *administrator* who acts when there was no *will* and the *executor* who acts when there was a will.

PET   Abbreviation for *potentially exempt transfer*.

Potentially exempt transfer (PET)   A gift between individuals or a gift between an individual and a *trust*, other than a *discretionary trust*, made during the lifetime of the giver. There is no *inheritance tax* charge on the gift provided the giver survives for seven years. If they do not, the PET is reassessed as a *chargeable transfer* and tax may then be due after all.

Purchased life annuity   An investment whereby you hand over a lump sum to an insurer, which then pays you an income for life. You cannot get back your investment in the form of a lump sum, but part of each regular payment to you is deemed to be return of your capital – the rest is deemed to be income. The capital element of each payment does not count as income for tax purposes, so there is no income tax on that part and it cannot be used to make 'regular payments out of income' under the IHT rules (see p. 54).

Registered charity   A charity listed on the Register of Charities kept by the Charity Commissioners. Registration tells you that the charity met the criteria for charitable status at the time it applied for registration, but should not be regarded as a 'seal of approval'.

Residuary gift   The gift under your will of whatever is left after all the *specific gifts* have been made, and debts and expenses (including tax) paid.

Residue   Whatever is left after all the *specific gifts* have been made, and debts and expenses (including tax) paid.

Retail Prices Index   The government index which tracks the general cost of living. Changes in the index give a widely used measure of inflation.

Reversionary interest   The right to the property in a trust at some specified time or on a specified occurrence, but not the right to income from or use of, the property before that time.

Settlor   The person who sets up a trust and puts money or assets into it.

Single premium life insurance bond   A type of investment whereby you use a lump sum to buy an insurance policy. The life cover element is low and the main aim of the policy is to provide investment growth. Special tax rules enable you to withdraw money periodically from the bond but to defer any liability for income tax on the withdrawals until later. These withdrawals do not count as income for the purpose of the 'regular payments out of income' exemption from IHT on gifts (see p. 54).

Specific gift   Gifts of money or things under a will. The gifts can be of various types: for example, a named item, a type of asset, a *pecuniary legacy* or a *demonstrative legacy*.

Tenancy in common   A method of jointly owning an asset, where you and the other owners have specified shares of the asset which you can sell or give away without the agreement of the other owners. On death, your share is given away in accordance with your *will* or the rules of *intestacy*.

Testator   The person (strictly, a man) who makes a *will*.

Testatrix   A woman who makes a *will*.

Trust   A legal arrangement whereby property is held by *trustees* on behalf of one or more *beneficiaries* to be used in accordance with the rules of the trust and trust law. Trusts can be very useful when making gifts as a way of giving assets but retaining some control over the way in which the assets are used; they are also useful if you wish to split the income and capital of assets and give each to a different person (or group of people).

Trustee   A person who is responsible for investing and distributing trust property in accordance with the rules of the trust and trust law. The trustees of a trust are the owners of the trust property but they hold it for the benefit of the *beneficiaries* and not their own use.

Variation   The process of changing the gifts made under a will after the *testator/testatrix* has died. This is achieved by a 'deed of variation' drawn up by one or more of the *beneficiaries*.

Whole life policy   A type of life insurance policy designed to pay out on the death of the policyholder whenever that might occur. Policies can also cover more than one person with payment due on either the first of second death.

Will   A legal document specifying how your *estate* is to be distributed and to whom at the time of death.

Useful addresses

Gifts to charities

The Charity Commission for England and Wales
57–60 St Albans House,
Haymarket, London
SW1Y 4UX
071-210 4556

The Charity Commission for England and Wales
Graeme House, Derby Square,
Liverpool L2 7SB
051-227 3191

The Charity Commission for England and Wales
Woodfield House, Tangier,
Taunton, Somerset TA1 4BL
TAUNTON (0823) 345000

Copies of the Central Register of Charities are also kept at Birmingham, Bristol, Mold, Manchester, Newcastle upon Tyne, Norwich and York (see relevant phone book for details) and can be inspected by the public.

Inland Revenue
(for charities in England, Wales and Northern Ireland)
Charity Division, St John's House, Merton Road, Bootle,
Merseyside L69 9BB
051-472 6000

Inland Revenue
(for charities in Scotland)
Trinity Park House, South Trinity Road, Edinburgh EH5 3SD
031-551 8127

The Charities Aid Foundation
48 Pembury Road, Tonbridge,
Kent TN9 2JD
TONBRIDGE (0732) 771333

National Council for Voluntary Organisations (NCVO)
(for England)
26 Bedford Square, London
WC1B 3HU
071-636 4066

Scottish Council for Voluntary Organisations (SCVO)
19 Claremont Crescent,
Edinburgh EH7 4QD
031-556 3882

Northern Ireland Council for Voluntary Action (NICVA)
127 Ormeau Road, Belfast
BT7 1SH
BELFAST (0232) 321224

Wales Council for Voluntary Action (WCVA)
Llysifor, Crescent Road,
Caerphilly CF8 1XL
CAERPHILLY (0222) 869224

Gifts to family and friends

Capital Taxes Office (England & Wales)
Minford House, Rockley Road,
London W14 0DF

Capital Taxes Office (Northern Ireland)
Doncaster House, 52–58 Great
Victoria Street, Belfast BT2 7BB
BELFAST (0232) 236633

Capital Taxes Office (Scotland)
Mulberry House, 16 Picardy
Place, Edinburgh EH1 3NF

Local tax offices and Tax Enquiry
Centres: refer to local telephone
directories under 'Inland
Revenue'.

BIBLIOGRAPHY

Bowen, N. 1991. *Tolley's tax legislation 1991–92: inheritance tax*. Croydon, Tolley

Capital Taxes Office. 1991. *IHT1: Inheritance tax*. London, Inland Revenue

Charities Aid Foundation (CAF). 1990. *Charity Trends*. 13th edn. Tonbridge, CAF

Charities Aid Foundation. 1991. *Charity Trends*. 14th edn. Tonbridge, CAF

Charities Aid Foundation. 1992. *Individual giving and volunteering in Britain*. 5th edn. Tonbridge, CAF

Chatterton, D. A. 1990. *Wills*. 2nd edn. London, Longman

Inland Revenue. January 1990. *Independent taxation: a guide for tax practitioners*. London, Inland Revenue

Inland Revenue. 1993. Budget press releases

Inland Revenue. 1991. *Trusts*. Consultative document. London, Inland Revenue

Noakes, B. and Savory, S. 1991. *Capital gains tax 1991–92*. Croydon, Tolley

Noakes, B. and Savory, S. 1991. *Inheritance tax 1991–92*. Croydon, Tolley

Price Waterhouse. 1993. *Estate Planning*. Croydon, Tolley

Ray, R. and Redman, J. 1989. *Practical inheritance tax planning*. London, Butterworth

Tolley. 1993. *Taxation*. Various issues

Turner, R. T., Hurst, K. B. and Burgess, A. C. 1990. *Charities Manual*. 3rd edn. Croydon, Tolley

INDEX

accumulation-and-maintenance
  trusts 99, 157
  example 100
  rules governing 99
  taxation of 106-7
  time limit on 99
addresses 167-8
administrator, meaning of term
  112, 157
affinity cards 42-3, 157
agricultural property relief 71,
  84, 138
allowable business expense
  charity donation as 41
  children's earnings as 94
  meaning of term 157
assets
  giving to charity 35-6, 45
  meaning of term 50, 157
  ownership of, tax position of
    couples affected by 88-90
  tax on 50, 53
associated operations 147-8

beneficiary, meaning of term 95-6,
  112, 157
bequests, charity donation 36
bibliography 169
birthday presents 56
Business Expansion Scheme (BES)
  52, 158
business property relief 137-8
  assets qualifying for 137

business qualifying for 138
  example calculation 137
businesses
  gifts from 41-2
  giving away 70-1, 83-4
  passing on 137-8, 147

capital gains, reporting to tax
  office 71
capital gains tax (CGT) 49-53, 158
  calculation of liability 60-4, 68
    examples 69-70
  chargeable gain calculated 60,
    62-3
    examples 60-2, 63-4
  example 51
  hold-over relief for 70-1
  indexation allowance for 60,
    64-8
  liability on assets acquired after
    April 1982 60-2
  liability on assets acquired before
    April 1982 62-4
  liability for trusts 101, 102, 103,
    105, 106
  rates of 64-5, 158
  reduction of liability 59-60
  scope of 50-2
  tax-free transactions 52-3, 158
  time to be paid 72
Capital Taxes Office, addresses 168
capital transfer tax (CTT) 12, 74
  see also inheritance tax

chargeable gains
  calculation of 60, 62-3
    examples 60-2, 63-4
  reporting to tax office 71
chargeable transfers
  meaning of term 74, 158
  reporting to tax office 84-5
  running total of 74, 80, 127
  tax-free slice 74, 127, 155-6
    use on death 142-3
  taxation of 74-5, 126
    examples 76-8
  trust gifts as 103
charitable bequests 36, 45
charitable trusts 38-41, 45, 100,
  158-9
  example 39-40
  rules governing 40
charities
  administration costs 22-3
  amount given 9, 29, 32, 34
  checking on 21
  choosing of 17-23
  definition 18
  giving to 9-10, 15-46
    non-crash gifts 35-6
    other ways of giving 35-43
    summary of methods 45
    tax-efficient schemes 25-34,
      36-42
  meaning of term 17-19
  money spent by 22-3
  registration of 20, 164
  tax benefits for 25-6
  tax position 25-6, 52, 53
  VAT paid by 25-6
Charities Aid Foundation (CAF)
  21, 159
  address 167
  Charity Account 36-8, 45, 159
    charges for 37
charity collections, checking on
  20-1
Charity Commission 20, 21, 22,
  39, 159
  address 167

chattels
  CGT liability 50
  meaning of term 50, 159
  surviving spouse's entitlement to
    113
cheques, gift by 151
children
  capital gains tax entitlements 92
  definition 55, 115, 159
  entitlement if no will 115-16,
    119
  friendly society plans for 91-2
  gifts to 90-3
    covenants used 93-4
    from friends and relatives 93
    from parents 90-2
    National Savings Bonus Bonds
      for 91
    tax-free income for 91
Christmas presents 56
codicil, meaning of term 121,
  159
covenants
  charitable giving by 26-31, 45,
    159
  deed of covenant 26-30
  examples 27, 30-1
  gifts to children by 93-4, 159
  length of time for 28, 30
  loan covenant 30-1, 45
  rules governing 29
  wording of 28
  see also deed…; loan…
credit card/charity link-ups 42-3
currency, CGT liability 50, 51

death
  alteration of will after 150-3
  tax payable on 125-40
    lifetime gifts 78, 125-7
deathbed gifts 150
decreasing term insurance 149
deed of covenant 26-30
  example 27
deeds of variation 152, 165
  example calculation 152

proposed changes 152-3
demonstrative legacy 122, 159
deposited deed/covenant: *see* loan covenant
disabled trusts 100, 159-60
disclaimers 152, 160
discretionary trusts 38, 45, 98
  calculation of IHT, examples 76-7, 80-1
  definition 97, 98, 160
  example 98-9
  gifts with reservation to 81-3
  IHT reduced by using 145, 146
  taxation of 103-6
    example 104
    proposed changes 105-6
  see also accumulation-and-maintenance...; charitable...; disabled trusts
domicile, meaning of term 53
donatio mortis causa 151

endowment policy 150
estate
  meaning of term 36, 127, 160
  reducing size of 150
  tax on 127
  valuation of 127
estate duty 12
  see also inheritance tax
executor, meaning of term 112-13, 160

family businesses
  gifts from 42
  giving away 70-1, 83-4
  passing on 137-8, 147
family provision claim (from estate) 118, 125, 160
farms, IHT relief on 71, 83-4, 139
fixed-interest trusts: *see* interest-in-possession trusts
foreign currency, CGT liability 51
forms (Inland Revenue)
  chargeable transfers 84
  Gift Aid scheme 32

jointly owned assets 89
free estate 127
free-of-tax gifts 128, 130-1, 143
  example calculation 131-2
  mixed with taxable gifts 132
friendly society plans 160
  children's savings 91-2

gardens, CGT liability 50-1
generation skipping 145
Gift Aid scheme 31-2, 45, 161
  example 32
  Inland Revenue form required 32
  minimum allowable 31
gifts
  lifetime
    capital gains tax on 59-71
    to charities 25-43
    to family and friends 47-108
    inheritance tax on 73-85
  see also lifetime gifts
gifts under will 128-36
gifts with reservation 81-3
  IHT planning by using 144-5
  meaning of term 81-2, 160-1
glossary 157-65
gross covenants 29
gross gifts
  calculation of IHT on 75
    example 77
  meaning of term 74
grossing up (of free-of-tax gifts) 131, 132, 161
  example calculations 131, 133, 135

higher-rate taxpayers
  charity donations 27, 30, 31
  covenants 27, 30, 93
hold-over relief (for CGT) 70-1, 161
home
  CGT liability 50-1
  giving away 83
housing associations, gifts to 54

husband/wife
    entitlement if no will 113-14,
        118
    gifts between 52, 53, 55, 56,
        87-90

income tax 161
    and gifts 87-94
    liability for trusts 101, 105, 106
independent taxation 87-8, 161-2
indexation allowance (CGT) 60,
    64-8, 162
indexation factor, calculation of
    64-8
inflation
    capital gains due to
        CGT liability 62
        indexation allowance for 60,
            64-8
    retail price index for 64, 65
inheritance 109-53
inheritance planning 141-53
    aims of 141-2
    gifts on death 142-3, 150
    insurance used 148-51
    lifetime gifts used 143-5
    loans used 147
    trusts used 145-7
Inheritance (Provision for Family
    and Dependants) Act (1975)
    118, 125
inheritance tax (IHT) 53-7, 162
    by whom payable 74, 78, 79,
        139
    examples 55-6, 76-7, 80-1
    expenditure-out-of-income
        exemption 54-5, 82, 144, 148
    fall-in-value relief for 126
    liability for trusts 101, 102,
        103-4, 106
    on lifetime gifts 73-85
    potentially exempt transfers 53,
        57, 73, 79-80
    rates of 74, 78, 80, 125, 155-6
    reduction of 40, 141-53
    scope of 53, 74
    tax-free gifts 53-6, 128, 129
    when payable 84-5, 139
    yearly tax-free exemption 55, 82,
        144, 148
    see also chargeable transfers;
        gross...; net gifts
Inland Revenue
    chargeable transfers reported 84
    Charity Division, address 167
    forms 32, 84, 89
insurance policy premiums, IHT
    freedom 54, 148, 150
insurance policy proceeds
    CGT liability 52
    paid into trust 148-9
interest in possession, definition 97,
    162
interest-in-possession trusts 97
    definition 97, 162
    IHT reduced by using 146-7
    taxation of 101-3
        example 102
        proposed changes 103
intestacy
    entitlement of children 115-16,
        119
    entitlement of husband/wife
        113-14, 118
    examples 114, 116, 117
    meaning of term 113, 162
    no near relatives 116-18
    partial 118
    problems caused by 111-12,
        118-19
investments, CGT liability 51-2

joint tenancy 89, 163
jointly owned assets 88-90

legacies 122
life insurance
    IHT reduced by using 148-51
    PETs protected from IHT 81,
        149
    premiums as tax-free gifts 54,
        148, 150

proceeds paid into trust 148-9
protection from IHT using 81
life interest, meaning of term 115, 163
life-interest trusts: *see* interest-in-possession trusts
lifetime gifts
  capital gains tax on 59-71
  IHT-free gifts 54-6
  IHT reduced by using 143-5
  inheritance tax on 73-85
  tax on death within seven years 78
  tax office to be informed 71, 84-5
  to charities 25-43
  to family and friends 47-108
limited companies, gifts from 41, 42
loan covenant 30-1, 45, 163
  example 30
  minimum amount feasible 31
loans, IHT reduced by making 147
lump-sum gifts, charity donations 30, 31-2, 45

maintenance payments 55
marriage settlement 56
mentally incapacitated person's affairs, trust to administer 100, 159-60
money, CGT liability 50, 51
motor vehicles, CGT liability 51
museums, gifts to 52, 57

National Savings investments 163
  Children's Bonus Bonds 91
net covenants 29
net gifts
  calculation of IHT on 75
    example 75-7
  meaning of term 74
non-cash donations to charity 35-6, 45
non-taxpayers
  charity donations 29, 32

covenants 29, 93
ownership of assets, tax position of couples affected by 88-90

Payroll Giving schemes 33-4, 36-8, 45, 163
  example 33
  maximum allowable 33
pecuniary legacy 122, 163
Personal Equity Plan (PEP) 52, 163
personal representative, meaning of term 112, 164
political aspects of charities 19
political parties, gifts to 54
potentially exempt transfers (PETs) 53, 57, 73, 79-80, 164
  insurance to pay IHT bill 81, 149
  taxation of 80-1, 125, 126
  trust gifts as 101
public benefit gifts 52, 54, 57
purchased life annuity 54, 164

quick succession relief 136-7

reading list 169
registered charities 20, 164
relatives
  entitlement if no will 116-18
  lifetime gifts to 47-108
reservation, gifts with 81-3, 160-1
residuary gifts 122, 128, 164
Retail Prices Index (RPI) 64, 164
  values listed 65
reversionary interest (in a trust) 97, 102, 164
rising-value gifts, IHT planning by using 144
running total (of chargeable transfers) 74, 79, 127

self-employed persons, gifts from 41, 42
settlements: *see* trusts
settlor, meaning of term 95, 164

shares
  business property relief on 138
  CGT liability 66-8
small-gift IHT exemption 56
special schemes
  charitable giving 25-34
    advantages for donors 26-32
specific gifts 121-2, 165
  free-of-tax gifts 130-1
  tax-bearing gifts 129-30
  tax-free gifts 129
sterling currency, CGT liability 50
stocks 158
  CGT liability 52, 66-8
students, income from parents 93,
  94

tax-bearing gifts 128, 129-30, 143
  example calculations 130, 132-6
tax-free gifts 53-6, 128, 129
  example calculation 129
  IHT reduced by using 144
  to charities 25-34
  to family and friends 49-58
temporary charitable trust 40
tenancy in common 89, 165
term insurance 149
testator/testatrix, meaning of term
  112, 165
trustee, meaning of term 96, 165
trusts 13, 95-107
  charitable giving by 38-40, 100
  choice of type 96-7
  IHT reduced by using 145-7
  lifetime gifts to 101, 103, 106,
    145
  meaning of term 95, 165
  participants in 95-6, 97, 98, 99
  purposes of 96
  set-up in wills 97, 98, 146-7
  taxation of 100-7
  types of 97-107
  see also accumulation-and-
    maintenance...; charitable...;
    disabled...; discretionary...;
    interest-in-possession trusts

unit trusts, CGT liability 66-8
Unlisted Securities Market (USM)
  shares, relief on 138

Value Added Tax (VAT), paid by
  charities 25-6
variation of will (after death)
  150-3, 165
voluntary groups 17-18, 21
  National Councils for 167-8

wealth
  distribution in UK 10-12
  taxation of transfer 12-13, 53-7
    see also inheritance tax
wedding gifts 56
whole life policy 150
will
  alteration after death 150-3
    example calculation 152
  codicil to 121
  drawing up of 119-20
  dying without 113-19
    problems arising 111-12,
      118-19
    survival by children 115-16
    survival by husband/wife
      113-14
    survival by no near relatives
      116-18
    see also intestacy...
  exclusion of dependants in 123
  gifts under 128-36
    example calculations 129, 130,
      131-2
  legacies from 122
  making gifts in 121-2
  meaning of term 111, 165
  quality of 120
  renewal of 120-1
  residuary gifts from 122
  revoking of 120, 121
  specific gift in 121
  terminology used 112-13
  trust set up in 97, 98, 146-7
will-writing firms 120